COMPACT
CYMRU

Plac

Brecon Beacons

Malcolm Llywelyn

Gwasg Carreg Gwalch

First published in 2018
© text: Malcolm Llywelyn
© images: Visit Wales/Gwasg Carreg Gwalch
© Crown copyright (2017) Visit Wales
© publication: Gwasg Carreg Gwalch 2018

ISBN: 978-1-84524-275-6
Cover design: Eleri Owen; map: Alison Davies

Published by Gwasg Carreg Gwalch,
12 Iard yr Orsaf, Llanrwst, Wales LL26 0EH
tel: 01492 642031
email: books@carreg-gwalch.cymru
website: www.carreg-gwalch.cymru

Preface by the author

I was born and raised in Merthyr Tudful where I learnt Welsh as an adult. Following my retirement, my wife and I came to live in a little village just outside the market town of Brecon, where we have happily remained for the last 20 years.

Some years ago I joined the board of our local *papur bro*, *Fan a'r Lle* (Welsh community quarterly) for which I write a piece on our area and also a page for Welsh learners. As a Welsh learner myself I am keen to support others and to that end have published several books for learners. I have also published 3 books on place-names in Merthyr Tudful and Breconshire.

Page 1: Ysgyryd Fawr from Blorens; below: Craig y Nos; opp.: Cascades on Nedd Fechan

Cynnwys

Introduction

Place names can describe a natural feature of an area such as a mountain, hill, field, river or brook and places of habitation including settlements, villages and farms. The name may also refer to a person of historical or local importance and an event in history. In this book we will consider the place names of the Parc Cenedlaethol Bannau Brycheiniog/Brecon Beacons National Park. It became a designated National Park in 1957 and covers an area of 1.346 square kilometres or 520 miles from Gelli/Hay on Wye in the north to Cefn Coed y Cymer in the south and from Llandeilo in the west to Y Fenni/Abergavenny in the east. The Park includes four distinct mountain ranges, the highest being the Bannau Brycheiniog/Brecon Beacons, the Mynyddoedd Duon/Black Mountains, the Fforest Fawr/Great Forest and the Mynydd du/Black Mountain. The purpose of the National Park is to protect and promote the natural features, wildlife and cultural heritage of the Brecon Beacons to be enjoyed and appreciated by its many visitors.

The vast majority of place names in the Brecon Beacons National Park are in the Welsh language. Brecon is derived from Brycheiniog which in Welsh means the land of Brychan, who was a saint of Irish origin and ruled the area in the fifth century. The kingdom of Brycheiniog emerged in early 400 AD following the end of the Roman occupation of the lands of south Wales. The land of Brycheiniog was situated in the valleys of the Llynfi and the Usk and extended in the north from the border with Builth to Gwent and Morgannwg in the south.

The aim of the book is to translate or explain the meaning of place names and to note any information of historical or cultural interest. The list of place names is taken from ordnance survey maps of the Brecon Beacons National Park. place names are in alphabetical order with the translation from Welsh to English in italics followed by any information known about meaning or historical interest and English names in brackets, ending with the Ordnance Survey grid reference.

Wild ponies on the Brecon Beacons

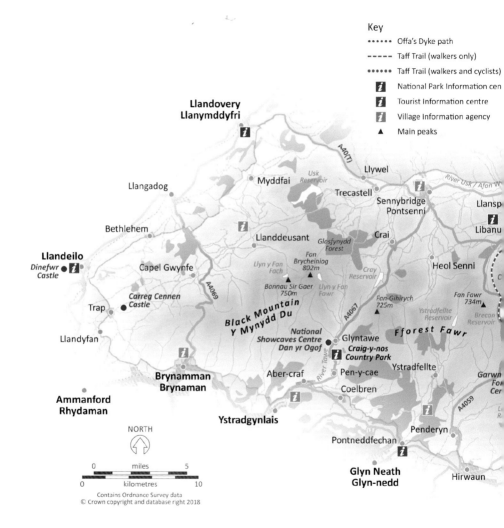

Pronunciation in Welsh

The seven vowels in Welsh can be long or short.

a	long as in	half and short as	ram
e		late	met
i		seed	sit
o		floor	not
u		need	sit
w		school	book
y		pun	knit

Consonants

c	king
ch	loch
dd	this
f	very
ff	fork
g	game
ng	song
ll	as in Llanelli
ph	photo
r	red (with a trill)
rh	(trilled with h)
s	same
th	think

Words in Welsh with more than one syllable the stress usually falls on the penultimate syllable. Gender is used in Welsh and a mutation follows the definite article; y, yr, 'r (the). For example: carreg (stone) – y garreg (the stone); draenen (thorn) – y ddraenen (the thorn); carn (cairn) – y garn (the cairn). Adjectives mutate after a feminine noun; du (black) mutates to ddu in nant ddu; mawr (great or large) to fawr in fan fawr; coch (red) to goch in nant goch.

Llyn y Fan Fach

Parc Cenedlaethol Bannau Brycheiniog: A History of Place Names

Aber: *Mouth of the river: either a sea estuary or a confluence of two rivers*

Aber: A village at the confluence of the rivers Clydach and Caerfanell. The Caerfanell runs into Tal-y-bont reservoir. SO 1021.

Aberbrân: *Confluence of the rivers Brân and Usk.* Brân can mean crow or may describe a dark river. SN 9829.

Abercraf: *Mouth of the river Craf.* Tributary of the river Tawe. Craf is an old Welsh word for garlic which is now spelt garlleg in Welsh. (Abercrave). SN 8212.

Abercrai: *Mouth of the river Crai.* See entry for Crai. SN 8928.

Abercriban: *Mouth of the Criban – criban may mean a little ridge.* Site of a cairn and working quarry. SO 0612.

Abercynafon: *Mouth of river Cynafon.* Prefix cyn could mean pre/early – therefore, 'upper' river or 'head of the river'. Neolithic site. SO 0717.

Abercynrig: *Mouth of the river Cynrig.* See entry for Afon Cynrig. The river Cynrig joins the Usk below Abercynrig House.

The Abercynrig estate was granted to Sir Reginald Awbrey as a reward for his support by Bernard of Neufmarche in the 11th century. Bernard of Neufmarche was the Norman lord who built the castle in Brecon in 1093. The mansion house at Abercynrig was built by Sir William Awbrey in the 16th century. Following his death it was bought by John Jeffreys. The house and land was later purchased by Mr. John Lloyd of Dinas near Llanwrtyd in the 18th century and the house at Abercynrig was built by his son who named it 'Dinas' after his ancestral home. SO 0727.

Aberdyfnant: *Mouth of river Dyfnant.* Dyfn is an old Welsh word for dwfn which means deep and nant means stream or brook. SN 7725.

Abergwdi: *Confluence of the Gwdi.* Gwdi may derive from gwdenni, meaning to twist. SO 0227.

Aberhonddu: *Confluence of the rivers Honddu and Usk.* Aberhonddu is the Welsh

Crai reservoir

name for the town of Brecon. Honddu has been interpreted as meaning the easy or pleasant river. The castle in Brecon at the confluence of the Honddu and the Usk was built by Bernard of Neufmarche in 1093, the Norman lord who ruled the land of Brycheiniog until his death between 1123 and 1125. The Church of St. John, 'Priory of Brecon', was also built by Bernard of Neufmarche, which later became the Cathedral in 1923. The Priory and the monastic buildings, established by Roger of Battle, became the spiritual centre of Brycheiniog and marked the translation from Celtic to Norman worship. The castle was subjected to attack during the uprising of Llywelyn ap Gruffudd during the 13th century and the rebellion of Owain Glyndŵr in the early 15th century. SO 0428.

Dyffryn Crawnon

Aberysgir: *Confluence of the rivers Ysgir and Usk.* Ysgir may derive from esgair meaning a ridge or spur in mountain range. The ruins of a Norman castle built at the end of the 12th century or beginning of the 13th century by Bernard Fitz Unspac can be found here near the river Usk and opposite the ruins of the old Roman Fort. SO 0029.

Afon: *river*

Afon Aman: Aman may derive from amanaw, a variation of banw which means a pig or piglet and describes a river which burrows and roots its way through the ground. SN 7314.

Afon Brân: Could refer to Brân/Bendigeid-frân, the king of the Brythoniaid (southern Celtic Britain), from the mythical tales of the Mabanogi. SN 8030.

Afon Camnant: Cam is an adjective in

Afon Wysg at Crickhowell

Welsh meaning twisting or crooked. SN 6821.

Afon Clydach: Clydach is derived from the Irish cladach which means 'a stony shore or a river flowing over a stony bed.' SN 7419.

Afon Crai: Fresh or raw flowing river. SN 8823.

Afon Crawnon: Crawnon derives from crafnant and craf is an old Welsh word for garlleg, namely garlic. SO 1218.

Afon Cynrig: River from highest point. Cynrig derives from 'cyn' meaning head, chief or highest point, 'rhig' is a stream or current from the latin 'rigo' which means to flow, a brook. Cynrig is also derived from the personal noun Cynwrig or Cynfrig which was anglicised to the modern surname Kendrick. The source of the Cynrig is Nant Sere in Cwm Sere below Pen y Fan – the highest point. SO 0625.

Afon Dringarth: Dring is an old Welsh word for ascent or slope and garth means hill or ridge. SN 9416.

Afon Ebw: Eb may derive from ebol which means colt or horse and w from wy which describes land or territory. SO 1513.

Afon Gïedd: Gïedd probably derives from cïaidd which means brutal, savage or fierce. SN 8220.

Afon Gwydderig: The river is near a prominent stone or cairn and is a tributary of afon Brân. SN 7834.

Afon Haffes: Haffes derives from hafesb (haf – summer, hesb – dry). SN 8317.

Afon Hepste: Hepste derives from hesb meaning a tendency to dry and teu which refers to darkness. The source of the Afon Hepste is on the southern slopes of Fan Fawr and it flows into Afon Mellte – a tributary of the Afon Nedd. SN 9411.

Afon Hydfer: Hydfer may derive from hyder which can mean reliance – could be 'a reliant flowing river'. SN 8526.

Afon Llechach: Llechach probably derives from llechog meaning rocky – a rocky, stoney river.. SN 7825.

Afon Llia: Llia derives from llapu which means to lap. SN 9216.

Afon Mellte: Mellte may derive from mellt or mellten which means lightning – a fast flowing river. SN 9211.

Afon Mihartach: *Mihartach river.* SN 7822.

Afon Pyrddin: *River by the striking fortress; or sweet flowing river.* SN 8809.

Afon Sawdde: Sawdde may derive from suddo which means to sink – the flow sinks into crevices or through limestone. Source of the river is Llyn y Fan Fach and

Sgŵd Uchaf Clun-gwyn on Afon Mellte

it is a tributary of the Tawe. SN 7323.

Afon Sgio: Sgio or ysgio may originate from the 14th century recorded name 'yskenac', which may derive from Ysgaw, elder trees in Welsh or the Irish 'seach' which means whitethorn. SN 8028.

Afon Sychlwch: Sychlwch is a dry pool or inlet. SN 8022.

Afon Taf Fawr: Taf may derive from a word meaning to flow. Mawr (fawr) meant great/greater. The Taf Fawr rises below Corn Du and flows through the three reservoirs, the Beacons, Cantref and Llwyn Onn. SO 0209.

Afon Tarell: Tarell is an old obscure word for spring source. The Tarell rises below Pen y Fan and joins the river Usk at Llanfaes in Brecon. SN 9722.

Afon Tawe: Tawe is a dark or flowing river. SN 8419.

Afon Twrch: Twrch is boar in Welsh and probably refers to a river burrowing through the land. SN 7717.

Afon Wysg: River Usk. It is thought that wysg may derive from the old Celtic words, peisg or eisc and the Latin piscis, which means fish – a river full of fish. SN 8528.

Afon y Cwm: *The valley river.* SN 8232.

Afon y Waun: Waun is a meadow or a moor river. SN 9716.

Allt: hillside or slope (usually wooded)

Allt Aber-brân-fawr: See entries for Aberbrân and Afon Brân. SN 9928.

Allt Caeau-bychan-mawr: The last part means great little fields hill. SN 7125.

Allt Cefntelych: An area across a low ridge of pasture land near Myddfai. Telych is an obscure word and its meaning is not known. SN 7933.

Allt Cwmnantybeudy: Locally pronounced as Cwmnantboidy, similar to Llanboidy. The name beudy means cowshed and the hillside probably refers to the old custom of taking cattle from the lowland winter quarters to upland pastures for the summer. SN 7930.

Allt Cwmtawel: Tawel is quiet or peaceful. SN 6819.

Allt Ddu: Du is dark or black. SO 0224.

Allt Fach: Fach is small SN 8417.

Allt Fawr Esgairllaethdy: Esgair is a ridge; llaethdy is a dairy. SN 7829.

Allt Feigan: F(M)eigan: personal name. SO 0923.

Allt Forgan: F(M)organ: personal name. SO 0617.

Dyffryn Wysg

Allt Glynyroddod: Could derive from 'yr hyrddod' (rams). SN 7834.

Allt Gwernfelin: Gwern: alder; f(m)elin: mill. SN 7933.

Allt Llannerch Goch: Llannerch: glade; g(c)och: red. SN 8132.

Allt Llwynpiod: Llwyn: bush; piod: magpies.SN 8133.

Allt Lwyd: Llwyd – grey. Hill overlooking Talybont reservoir. SO 0818.

Allt Nant Ioroth: Hillside at 'Ioroth' stream. SN 7729.

Allt Pant y Grafog: Pant: hollow. 'Grafog' may derive from 'craf', Welsh for wild garlic. SN 7224.

Allt Pen y Graig-goch: Pen: head; Graig-goch: Red rock. SN 7422.

Allt Rhyd y gwartheg: Rhyd: ford; gwartheg: cattle. SN 7220.

Allt Troedrhiwfelin: *Slope at the foot of the mill hill.* SN 7833.

Allt Twyn y Fan Fach: Twyn: hillock; Fan Fach: small peak. SN 7931.

Allt y Carw: Carw: deer. SN 7728.

Allt y Dagfa: D(t)agfa: narrow stretch of a path (lit. - 'traffic jam'!) SN 8132.

Allt y Fedw: F(b)edw – birch. SN 7225.

Allt y Ferdre: F(a)erdref – home farm. SN 8033.

Allt y Fergwm: F(b)ergwm: short valley. SN 8132.

Allt y Geifr: Geifr – goats. SN 7628.

Allt y Gog: Gog: cuckoo. SN 7834.

Allt y Gwydre: Gwydre: the name of a farm at nearby Llanddeusant. SN 7927.

Allt Ynysbordau: Ynysbordau: tables (raised) field. SN 7935.

Allt yr Esgair: Esgair: ridge. The summit is the site of an Iron Age fort built between 800BC and the arrival of the Romans here in the AD70s. The Roman road between the fort Y Gaer at Brecon and Gobannium at Abergavenny runs along the ridge. SO 1224.

Allt yr Hafod Fawr: Hafod Fawr: great summer dwelling. SN 8031.

Alltysgoedreddfin: Goedreddfin – great wood. SN 8431.

Aman Fach: F(b)ach: little. See entry for Afon Aman. SN 7416.

Aman Fawr: F(m)awr: big. SN 7516.

Arhosfa'r Garreg-lwyd: *The grey rock abode.* The site of a Roman camp, a campaign base and marching camp. SN 8026.

Banc: bank

Banc Celynnog: Celynnog: holly-grove. SN 7023.

Banc Crucorfod: Crucorfod: forced mound. SN 6715.

Banc Melyn: Melyn – yellow. SN 7019.

Banc Pen-Arthur: Pen Arthur: Arthur's head/summit. SN 7123.

Banc Wernwgan: Wernwgan: Gwgan's alder grove. Gwgan is the name of a historical figure in Ceredigion. It is an area of moorland and was once the site of limestone quarries. SN 6818.

Banc y Cerrig Pwdron: Cerrig: stones. Pwdron may derive from pwdr, meaning to decay or 'layabouts/robbers'. SN 7118.

Ban/Fan: high peak/beacon

Bannau Brycheiniog: *Beacons or peaks of Brycheiniog – the land of Brychan.* SN 9820.

Bannau Sir Gaer: *Carmarthenshire beacons.* SN 8021.

Banwen Gwŷs: *Pig's marshland.* Banwen may derive from 'panwaun', meaning marshland and gwŷs is an obscure Welsh word for pig – mochyn. SN 8019.

Banwen Gwythwch: *Wild pig marshland.* Gwythwch is an obscure Welsh word for wild pig. SN 6717.

Bedd: grave

Bedd Llywarch: Llywarch is an ancient Welsh personal name. Site of menhir – standing stones. SN 9616.

Beddau'r Derwyddon: Derwyddon: druids. The site of pillow mounds, an artificial warren built in medieval times to breed rabbits. SN 6718.

Bethlehem: *Biblical chapel.* The name of this small hamlet derived from the Congregational chapel built in 1800. SN 6825.

Betws: *Prayer-house or chapel-of-ease.* SO 2919.

Blaen: source of river/head of a valley/cwm

Blaen Caerfanell: Caerfanell which translates as 'fanell fort' is the name of the river and a waterfall. The river is a tributary of the Usk. SO 0519.

Blaen Crai: Crai has been interpreted as meaning fresh flowing river. SN 8720.

Blaen Crew: Crew: clamorous stream. The stream flows into the Cantref Reservoir. SO 0019.

Blaen Cwm Banw: Banw: piglet. SO 0722.

Blaen Dringarth: Dringarth: mountain slope. SN 9416.

Bannau Sir Gaer and Llyn y Fan Fach

Blaen Dyar: Dyar is an oscure Welsh word for loud or noise. SO 2312.

Blaen Dyffryn Crawnon: Dyffryn: valley; Crawnon – place of wild garlic. SO 0914.

Blaen Glais: *Stream at the head of the valley.* SO 0310.

Blaen Gloddfa-fawr: Gloddfa fawr: great quarry. SO 0314.

Blaen Grwyne Fawr: *Source of the Crwyne Fawr river.* SO 2032.

Blaen Llia: *Source of the Llia stream – Llia (Llio) is probably a personal name.* SN 9316.

Blaen Nant y Bedd: Nant: stream; bedd: grave. SO 2427.

Blaen Senni: *Source of the Senni river.* Senni may derive from the personal name Sannon, who was a seventh century Irish saint and bishop and a friend of St. David. SN 9119.

Blaen Taf Fechan: *Source of the little Taf river.* Taf originates from Brythonic, the Celtic language from which Welsh evolved, and refers to the flow or darkness of the water. The river joins the Upper Neuadd Reservoir. SO 0120

Blaen y Clychau: Clychau: upland bells. SN 7618.

Blaen y Glyn: Glyn: narrow valley. Site of waterfalls and Cadw listed round cairn. SO 0519.

Blaenbychlyd: Bychlyd may derive from bwlch – *gap* and llydan – *broad*. SO 1421.

Blaencib: *Head of basin/crater.* SN 6721.

Blaenllynfell: *Source of river Llynfell.* SN 7618.

Blaenclydach: *Source of the river Clydach.* See afon Clydach. SN 7519.

Blaen-cwm: *Head of the valley.* SN 8913.

Blaenpedol: *Source of horseshoe stream.* Nant pedol and cwm pedol are on an old drovers route. Pedol is Welsh for horseshoe. SN 7117.

Blaentawe: *Source of the river Tawe.* Tawe may derive from the same source as taf meaning 'to flow'. SN 8422.

Blorens: *Windy hill.* The name may derive from the old English word 'blore' meaning a gust of wind. (Blorenge). SO 2611.

Brest: slope on the side of a hill

Brest Cwm Llwyd: Cwm llwyd: grey valley. Site of limestone quarries and kilns. SN 7019.

Brest Rhiw ddu: Rhiw ddu: black hill. SN 7219.

Brest Twrch: Twrch means wild boar and

probably refers to a burrowing river. The river Twrch rises in the Black Mountain. SN 8020.

Brest y Fan: Fan: ridge or peak. SN 9518.

Brest y Fedw: Y Fedw: birch trees. SN 7923.

Brest y Rhos: Rhos: moor. SN 7621.

Bronllys: *Brwyn's Court or Court of Rushes.* See Castell Bronllys SO 1435.

Bryn: *hill.* (see: SO 0722)

Bryn Arw: (G)arw – rugged. SO 3019.

Bryn Blaen-wysg: *At source of river Usk.* See entry for Afon Wysg. SN 8223.

Bryn Bugeiliaid: Bugeiliaid – Shepherds. SN 8613.

Bryn Cedni: Cedni may derive from an old Welsh word, *Cedny* the plural form of foxes. SN 7925.

Bryn Cefnog: Cefnog: harrow ridge. Site of shake hole which is a depression in limestone connecting with an underground passage. SO 0815.

Bryn Du: Du – black. SN 8625.

Bryn Elen: Elen probably relates to Sarn Helen, the Roman road which runs from Aberconwy in North Wales to Carmarthenshire in the South. Elen was princess of Segontium – Caernarfon – and wife of Macsen Wledig/Magnus Maximus, the Roman governor of Britain in the 4th century, featured in the Mabinogi. Bryn Elen is also the site of a round cairn. SN 8025.

Bryn Glas: Glas – blue or green. SO 0412.

Bryn Gwilym: *Gwilym's hill.* SN 9717.

Bryn Mawr: Mawr – big. SN 8024.

Bryn Melyn: Melyn – yellow. SN 9319. and SO 1018.

Bryn Merched: Merched – maidens. SN 8426.

Bryn Pentwyn-isaf: *Lower head of the dune hill.* SN 9516.

Bryn Pentwyn-uchaf: *Higher head of the dune hill.* SN 9517.

Bryn Pwllygerwn: *Pwll: pool; y gerwn is probably 'y gerwyn': cauldron.* SN 8127.

Bryn Teg: Teg – fair. SO 0222.

Bryn y Fuwch: Y fuwch: the cow. SN 8022.

Bryn yr ŵyn: Yr ŵyn: the lambs. SN 8026.

Bryn Gleision: Gleision – blue or green. SO 0715.

Buarth y Caerau: *Farmyard settlements.* Site of early Christian sculptured stone. SO 0713.

Bwlch ar y Fan between Pen y Fan and Corn Du

Bwlch: *pass/gap*

Bwlch ar y Fan: *Pass or gap on or near the summit.* Commonly known as 'the Gap'. SO 0320.

Bwlch Blaen Twrch: *Gap or pass at source of Twrch river.* See Brest Twrch. SN 8121.

Bwlch Bach ar Grib: *Little gap of the ridge.* SO 1830.

Bwlch Bryn rhudd: *Gap at brown hill.* The course of the failed attempt to establish a tramway through the Brecon Forest in the 19th century runs through this area. SN 8619.

Bwlch Cerrig Duon: *Gap at black rocks.* Site of stone circle, a round cairn, also known as maen mawr: *great stone.* SN 8522.

Bwlch Duwynt: Duwynt: black/bitter wind. SO 0020.

Bwlch Gwyn: Gwyn – white. SO 0316.

Bwlch y Deuwynt: Deuwynt: two winds. SN 7817.

Bwlch y Duwynt: Duwynt: black/bitter wind . SN 9019.

Bwlch y Gïedd: *The savage gap.* The name probably refers to the very steep slope of the pass. The footpath at Bwlch y Gïedd leads to the highest peak in the Black Mountain of Fan Brycheiniog. SN 8221.

Bwlch y Gors: The swamp at the mountain pass. SN 6922.

Bwlch: *Gap or pass.* Refers to the gap between Buckland Hill and Cefn Moel through which runs the route of the Roman road from Abergavenny to Brecon. SO 1421.

Bwlch y Dwyallt: Dwyallt: two wooded slopes. SO 0520.

Bwlch yr Efengyl: *Gospel Pass* SO 2334

Byfre Fechan: *Little highland stream.* 'Fre' may derive from bre, a Welsh word for hill or highland. The Byfre fechan travels downstream through Ogof Ffynnon Ddu and into the river Tawe. SN 8716.

Bylchau Blaenclydach: *Gaps at the source of the river Clydach.* The site of a standing stone (menhir). SN 8026.

Bylchau Rhos fain: *Gaps at the high narrow moorland.* SN 7517.

Cadair Fawr: *Great chair/mountain.* Probably refers to a glaciated mountain in the shape of a seat. It is also the site of a cairn and of one of the many limekilns in the area. SN 9712.

Cae Burdydd: *Field of the lords (Norman) or field of the short day.* It has also been described as, 'The field of slaughter'. Burdydd may derive from 'byrddydd' a

Bwlch yr Efengyl (Gospel Pass)

short day or an old Welsh word 'pyr' which means *lords*. This is reputed to be the burial place of the dead of the battle of Maes y Faenor, *Faenor field*. The place where a famous battle occurred in c 1290 between the two Norman lords, Gilbert de Clare, who built Morlais Castle, and Humphrey de Bohun, Lord of Brecknock. It is located close to the crossroads between Pontsarn and Pontsticill. A mound at Cae Burdydd, was excavated in 1823, in the presence of the Reverend Thomas Price, (Carnhuanwc), the Vicar of Cwmdu, and many human bones were found as well as the remains of iron weapons. SO 0410.

Caerfanell: *'Fanell' fort.* Manell is the name of the river. (M) changes to (F) in mutation. The river Caerfanell flows into Talybont Reservoir. SO 0616.

Camlas Sir Fynwy a Brycheiniog: *Monmouthshire and Brecon Canal.* The canal was originally opened between 1799 and 1800 to transport coal, lime and iron ore. It runs for 35 miles from the Brecon Basin along the Usk Valley to the Pontymoile Basin in Pontypool. The canal is now popular tourist attraction for cruising. SO 0428.

Canolfan Ymwelwyr y Parc Cenedlaethol: *National Parc Visitor Centre.* Opened in 1957 to provide information for visitors to the National Park. (Mountain Centre). SN 9726.

Cantref: *Hundreds. Hundred homesteads or settlements.* Cantref was an ecclesiatical parish from mediaeval times and a civil parish from the 16th century until 1974 when it became part of Llanfrynach Community Council. The term cantref referred to an administrative system of one hundred homesteads or settlements introduced by Hywel Dda, the well known legislator and ruler of South Wales. Cantref was part of Cantref Tewdos or Cantref Mawr. Tewdos was a son of the ancient ruler of Brycheiniog, Einon ap Gruffudd ab Elis. So 0223.

Cantref Church: *'Church of 1809'.* Originally dedicated to St. Cynidr, a 6th century saint and a grandson of Brychan Brycheiniog, the ancient ruler of Brecon and the surrounding area. The festival of St. Cynidr is on the 8th December. The church was rededicated to St. Mary c 1100 AD by the Normans and only in the past few years has the dedication to St. Cynidr been restored.

Castell Bronllys

Capel: *chapel*

Capel Gwynfe: Gwynfe: the white field. A village near Llangadog. SN 7221.

Capel Sant Mihangel: Sant Mihangel: St. Michael. SO 3318.

Capel y Ffin: Y Ffin: the boundary. An old chapel on the borders of Llandaf and St David's dioceses. Later an Anglican Benedictine monastery was established here by the Reverend Joseph Lynne, a monk called Father Ignatius (1837-1908). SO 2531.

Carn: *cairn*

Carn Caniedydd: Caniedydd: songster. May be descriptive of the whistling wind. It is the site of a Bronze Age cairn. SN 9815.

Carn Cennen: *Lichen cairn or cairn at the Cennen river.* Cennen could also be a personal name. SN 7018.

Carn Ddu: D(d)u: black. SO 0312.

Carn Fadog: Madog is a personal name. The last king of Powys was Madog ap Maredudd in the 12th century. It may also refer to Maen Madoc, a menhir or standing stone from the Bronze Age, inscribed in Latin during Roman times. SN 7617.

Carn Fatho: Fatho is a personal name. SN 7118.

Carn Fawr: *Great cairn.* SN 7018.

Carn Felen: Felen may derive from melyn, meaning Yellow. SO 0813.

Carn Goch: *Red cairn.* It is also known as Y Garn Goch or Garn Goch. The site of a significant Iron Age hill fort. The description of red probably refers to the colour of the hill of bracken in autumn. The memorial stone to Gwynfor Evans stands on the approach to Garn Goch. Gwynfor Evans (1912 – 2005) was the first member of parliament elected for Plaid Cymru in 1966. He was president of Plaid Cymru for 36 years. SN 6924.

Carn Nant Gwill Foel: *Stream at Gwilym's bare hill.* Gwill may be an abbreviation of the personal name Gwilym. SN 7920.

Carn Nant y Ddraenen: Nant y Ddraenen: thorn-bush stream. SN 7819.

Carn Pen Rhiw-ddu: *Cairn at the head of the black slope.* SN 7218.

Carn Pen y clogau: *Cairn at the top of the crags.* SN 7118.

Carn Pica: Pica: pointed. SN 7018; SN 7721; SO 0620.

Carn Pwll Mawr: Pwll mawr: great pool or hollow. SN 9511.

Carn y Botel: *The bottle cairn.* Bottle or bundle of hay or straw refers to the historical gathering of thin mountain hay. SN 9514.

Carn y Bugail: Bugail: shepherd. SO 0813.

Carn y Gigfran: Y gigfran: the raven. SN 7721.

Carn y Goetre: Y goetre: the settlement by the wood. SN 9414.

Carn yr arian: Yr arian: may refer to nant yr arian – the silvery stream. SN 9312.

Carn yr Helyg: Yr helyg: the willows. SO 0911.

Carn yr onnen: Yr onnen: the ash. SN 8816. Stone

Carn y Castell: *Cairn by the castle*. Site of a motte. SO 1529.

Carnau: *cairns*

Carnau Gwynion: Gwynion: white. SN 7320; SN 9214.

Carnau Gwŷs: *Cairns beside the river Gwŷs*. Gwŷs is an obscure word in Welsh for pig and it may translate as sow stream. SN 8120.

Carnau Llwydion: Llwydion: grey or holy. SN 7922.

Carnau Nant Menyn: *Cairns at the butter stream*. SN 7920.

Carnau'r Garreg Las: Garreg Las translates as blue rock. SN 7720.

Carno Reservoir: *Place of cairns*. May derive from 'carn' meaning stone cairn, an ancient burial site. SO 1613.

Carn-y-Gorfydd: Gorfydd may derive from gorfudd, an old word in Welsh for victorious. SO 2711.

Carreg: *stone/rock*

Carreg a'r Gap: *Stone on the gap*. SN 8215.

Carreg Cadno: Cadno – fox. SN 8715.

Carreg foel gam: *Bare rock step*. SN 7024

Carreg Goch: Goch – red. The wreckage of a Wellington bomber plane which crashed in 1944 with the loss of all six of the Canadian crew is to be found nearby. SN 8116.

Carreg Gorslwm: Gorslwm: bleak marsh. SN 9311.

Carreg Gywir: *The right or correct stone*. A boundary stone which may mark the northern boundary of the parish of Llanfoist. SO 2412.

Carreg Lem: *Sharp-edged crag*. SN 8017.

Carreg Lwyd: Llwyd – grey/holy. SN 7317; SN 8615.

Carreg Waun llech: *Rock on slab moor*. A striking menhir or standing stone sited high on Llangynidr Mountain. SO 1617.

Castell Dinas hillfort, Pengenffordd

Carreg wen Fawr y Rugos: *Great white rock on 'y Rugos'.* SO 1317.

Carreg yr Ogof: Yr ogof: the cave. SN 7721.

Carreg Cyn Ffyrdd: *Rock before the roads. Site of a standing stone.* SN 6722.

Carreglwyd: *Grey rock.* SN 6822.

Castell: *castle*

Castell Blaenllynfi: *Castle at the head of the river Llynfi.* The castle stood at the foot of Mynydd Llangors. It was captured by the Broases in 1215 and by Llywelyn Fawr in 1233. Llywelyn ap Gruffudd took the castle in 1262. It was eventually seized by the Crown and later fell into disrepair. SO 1422.

Castell Bronllys: *Brwyn's court or court of rushes castle.* Bron may derive from Brwyn – a personal name or brwyn which means rushes. The castle in Bronllys was the administrative centre of the Norman lord Walter Clifford in the 12th century. It was seized by Edward 11 during the 'Marcher Rebellion' in 1321. The castle became the property of Henry IV in 1399, it deteriorated and it was no longer habitable by 1521. The tower is now in the care of Cadw and it can be located half a mile, south-east of the village of Bronllys. SO 1434.

Castell Carreg Cennen: *Castle on the Cennen rock.* Cennen may derive from a personal name or refer to lichen or stoned river. The castle was built by Lord Rhys (Rhys ap Gruffudd) in the late 12th century. Lord Rhys was the prince of Deheubarth, the Kingdom of Dyfed and Brycheiniog. The castle changed hands many times following conflict between the Welsh and English. Owain Glyndŵr laid siege and failed to capture the castle in 1403. It was a Lancastrian stronghold during the War of the Roses in 1461. The castle was acquired by the Vaughan and Cawdor families and renovated in the 19th century. It is now privately owned as part of a farm and in the care of CADW. SN 6619.

Castell Coch: Coch: red. The castle was built from red sandstone and is also known as Castell Mellte which translates as *lightening castle or Mellteu a personal name.* The remains of the castle in Ystradfellte are found between afon Llia and afon Dringarth in the Beacons. It is understood the castle was held by William de Braose in 1239. SN 9314.

Castell Carreg Cennen

Castell y Geifr: Y geifr: the goats. SN 8216.
Castell Morlais: Morlais: loud stream. The castle was built by the Norman lord Gilbert de Clare in 1282. Gilbert de Clare, Earl of Gloucester and Lord of Glamorgan was a powerful Marcher Lord and commander of the English king's forces in south Wales. He also built Caerphilly Castle by 1270 as a defence against the onslaughts of Llywelyn ap Gruffudd. Morlais Castle was once owned by the Earl of Plymouth, who was a descendant of Ifor Bach. (Morlais Castle). SO 0409.

Cathedine: *Fortress of Cathed, a personal name.* The land of Cathedine was possessed by the Norman Lord Bernard de Neufemarche in the 11th century and It became part of the Norman Lordship of Blaenllyfni in the 12th century. It formed part of the Hundred of Talgarth following the Act of Union in 1536 and became the tithe parish of Cathedine in the 19th century. SO 1425.

Cefn: *ridge*
Cefn Bach: Bach: little. SN 9719; SO 0621.
Cefn Brynich: *Ridge of hill stream.* The Cefn Brynich Canal Bridge Acqueduct carries the Brecon and Mounmouthshire Canal over the Usk. It is a CADW listed building. SO 0727.

Cefn Cadlan: Cadlan may translate as battlefield, although there is no recorded history of a battle in this area. It is, however, the site an ancient settlement of prehistoric hut circles and burial cairns. SN 9611.

Cefn Cantref: *Ridge of Cantref.* See entry for Cantref. SO 0426.

Cefn Carn Fadog: *Ridge of Madog's cairn.* Site of a Bronze Age Barrow. SN 7616.

Cefn Coed y Cymer: '*The woody ridge of the confluence of the waters.*' A well known landmark in Cefn Coed is the 15 arch railway viaduct built in 1866, which crosses the Taf Fawr river. The bridge was designed with a curve to avoid land owned by the Crawshays'. The Unitarian chapel, Hen-dŷ-cwrdd – *the old meeting place* – was founded in 1747 in Cefn Coed. The chapel has been a centre of religious, educational and social influence. Edward Williams, the famous Iolo Morganwg, was a radical Unitarian and he attended a meeting at Hen-dŷ-cwrdd in 1802 as a member of the Welsh Unitarian Society. SO 0307.

Cefn Crew: *Clamorous ridge.* Nant crew

Cefn Golau cholera cemetary

has been translated as *clamorous stream*. Site of an ancient village settlement. SN 9919.

Cefn Cul: Cul: narrow. Site of ancient cairn and standing stone is nearby. SN 8519; SO 0119.

Cefn Cwm Llwch: *Ridge of valley lake*. See entry for Llyn Cwm Llwch. SO 0122.

Cefn Cyff: *Coffin ridge*. Cyff can also mean *stock* or *stump*. SO 0422.

Cefn Disgwylfa: *Ridge of look-out mountain*. SN 8123.

Cefn Edmwnt: Edmwnt is a personal name. SO 0720.

Cefn Esgair-carnau: Cairns at ridge of mountain spur. Barrow/cairn cemetery. SN 9814.

Cefn Mawr: Mawr: great. SN 7915.

Cefn Moel: Moel: bare. Site of round cairn. SO 1623.

Cefn Nant Lygos: Lygos probably derives from helygos an obscure Welsh word for helyg which means willows. SN 7923.

Cefn Nantygeugan: *Ridge of the stream at the hollow cairn*. SN 9914.

Cefn Perfedd: *Middle of ridge*. SN 9316; SN 9420.

Cefn Pwll-coch: Pwll coch: red pool. SO 1714.

Cefn Pyllauduon: Pyllau duon: black pools. SO 1012.

Cefn Rhudd: Rhudd: red. SN 8220.

Cefn Sychbant: Sychbant: dry valley. SN 9810.

Cefn Tarenni Cochion: Tarenni cochion: red escarpments. SO 0615.

Cefn Twrch: Twrch – boar. SN 8021.

Cefn y Cylchau: Cylchau: circles. Site of small cairn. SN 7519.

Cefn y Galchen: *The limestone ridge*. SO 2610.

Cefn y Garreg Las: *The blue stone ridge*. SN 7719.

Cefn y Parc: *Ridge at the open land or field*. SO 0028.

Cefn y Truman: Truman: headland. SN 7419.

Cefn Ynys-Fawr: Ynys Fawr: great water meadow. SO 0114.

Cefn yr Henriw: Henriw: old slope. SN 9718.

Cefn yr Ystrad: Yr ystrad: the vale. Site of cairns and limestone quarry worked in 18/19th century. SO 0713.

Cerrig: *stones/rocks*

Cerrig Edmwnt: *Edmwnt's stones*. SO 0619.

Coed Taf Fechan

Cerrig Mawr: *Large rocks.* SO 2906.

Cerrig y Llwyni: Y llwyni: the groves. SO 0612.

Ceunant Du: *Dark narrow gorge.* SN 9509.

Chwarel Ddu: *Dark quarry.* Site of limestone quarry in the 18/19th century. SO 2437.

Chwarel y Fan: *Quarry at the peak.* Site of a cairn. SO 2529.

Clawdd Coch: *Red dyke.* SO 0723.

Clo Cadno: Fox's crag. Clo may derive from clog an obscure Welsh word for crag or rock. Site of a cairn. SO 1116.

Clogau Mawr: *Great mine.* SN 7119.

Clydach: *Clydach is an Irish name for a river flowing on a flat stony bed.* It is the name of the river and the village. The site of ironworks originating in the 18th century and a limestone quarry. SO 2213.

Coed: *wood(s)*

Coed Aberllechach: *At the mouth of the stony brook.* SN 7524.

Coed Cae'r ebol: Cae'r ebol: colt's field. SO 0724.

Coed Cefngarreg: Cefn garreg: stone ridge. SN 7727.

Coed Craig Tŷ bach: Tŷ bach: little house. SO 1016.

Coed Cwm Iau: Iau is the Welsh word for yoke (here describing a yoke-shaped valley). It is also recorded on maps as Coed cwm iou. SO 3022.

Coed Cwmbrân: Cwm brân: crow valley. SN 8031.

Coed dan yr allt: Dan yr allt: below the hill. SN 7834.

Coed Dyffryn: Dyffryn – valley. SO 1916.

Coed Esgair Feithgen: *Wood at lichen-growing ridge.* SN 8031.

Coed Fenni-fach: *Wood at the lesser river by the smithies.* Site of an Iron Age hillfort and a tribal centre of the native tribe the Silures. SO 0129.

Coed Gïedd: Gïedd: savage or fierce. SN 8014.

Coed Glasfynydd: Glasfynydd – blue mountain. SN 8228; SN 8524.

Coed Godre'r waen: *Wood at the bottom of the meadow.* Waen may derive from gwaun which means moor or meadow. SN 7323.

Coed Llwyn y moch: Llwyn y moch: pig's grove. SN 9706.

Coed Nant y ceiliog: By the cock's stream. SO 0527.

Coed Peggy Shams: Peggy Shams is a personal name. SO 2905.

Near Corn Du summit

Coed Penmailard: Mailard may be a corruption moel allt which means *bare hill*. SO 0109.

Coed Pen-twyn: At the head of the dune. SN 9220.

Coed Penwyn: Penwyn: at the top of the white hill. SO 1916.

Coed Pen-y-rhiw: At the head of the hill. SN 7224.

Coed Perth y Piod: The magpie bush. SO 2216.

Coed Robin: Gadfly. SO 2823.

Coed Taf Fawr: *Great Taf wood*. The Brecon Beacons National Park visitors centre at Garwnant is situated in the Coed Taf Fawr. SN 9913.

Coed Tir Du: Dark land. SN 7623.

Coed Tŷ Canol: Middle house. SO 2824.

Coed Tŷ mawr: Great house. SN 9723.

Coed Tyle du: Black hill. SO 0723.

Coed Tylegarw: Wild hill. SN 9220.

Coed y Brenin: The king. SO 0623.

Coed y Caerau: The forts. The site of a large Iron Age fort. SO 0623.

Coed y Castell: The castle. SN 6719.

Coed y Cilau: Of the refuge. SO 1917.

Coed y Dorallt: At the hillside. SN 8529.

Coed y Fan: At the summit. SN 9422.

Coed y Gelli: The grove. SN 7422.

Coed y Prior: The prior's. SO 2910.

Coed y Rhaeadr: By the waterfall. SN 9011.

Coed y Wern: The alder-grove. SN 7630.

Coed y Wernfach: The little alder-grove. SO 1916.

Coed yr Allwys: *The wooded slope*. SO 2908.

Coed yr Eithin: The gorse. SO 1617.

Coedcae Du: *Dark woodfield – a field cleared of forest*. Coedcae or coedgae has a meaning which is particular to south Wales and describes, 'a wooded area on the steep upper slopes of the valleys.' SO 2906.

Coedwig Taf Fechan: *Little Taf forest*. SO 0416.

Coed-y-person: The parson's. SO 2713.

Coetgae Du: *Dark woodfield*. SO 0316; SO 1817.

Coetgae'r Gwartheg: *Cattle woodfield*. Site of summit cairns or prehistoric barrows – mounds of earth covering tombs. SO 0211.

Coetgae-llwyn: *Woodfield grove*. SO 0516.

Comen y Rhos: *Moorland common*. SN 8029.

Comin y Rhos: *Moorland common*. SN 9109.

Craig Gwaun Taf from Corn Du

Corgwm: *Dwarf valley.* SN 8329.

Corn Du: *Black pointed peak or stack.* Site of a Bronze Age cairn. Below Corn Du is the Tommy Jones Obelisk, a memorial to the 5 year old boy who died from exhaustion in 1900. The inscription on the memorial reads; 'This obelisk marks the spot where the body of Tommy Jones aged 5 was found. He lost his way between Cwmllwch farm and the Login on the night of August 4th 1900. After an anxious search of 29 days his remains were discovered Sept. 2nd. Erected by voluntary subscriptions. W. Powell Price Mayor of Brecon 1900.' SO 0021.

Cors y Beddau: *The graves marsh.* Site of prehistoric settlement. SN 9415.

Cradoc: Caradog Fraich-fras was a grandson of Brychan Brycheiniog and prince of Maesmynys – Mynys's field and Llanynys – church on the land beside a river. It is the site of a standing stone. SO 0130.

Crai: *Fresh or raw flowing river.* The village takes its name from the river Crai. The Llywel Stone was found at Crai. It has inscriptions in Latin and Ogham which indicates the association between the kingdom of Brycheiniog and Ireland. The original stone is kept at the British Museum. (Cray). SN 8924.

Craig: *rock/cliff/crag*

Craig Cerrig Gleision (**Gleisiad**): *Cliff by the rocky sewin/sea trout stream.* A National Nature Reserve. SN 9621.

Craig Cwm Cynwyn: At the head of white valley. SO 0220.

Craig Cwm Llwch: By the valley lake. SO 0021.

Craig Cwm Sere: *Sere valley crag.* Sere may be a personal name. SO 0121.

Craig Cwm-clyd: In the sheltered-valley. SN 7929.

Craig Cwmoergwm: In the cold valley. Cwm Oergwm is a Brecknock Wildlife Nature Rerserve. SO 0319.

Craig Danywenallt: Below the white wooded hillside. The location of the Danywenallt Youth Hostel. SO 1121.

Craig Ddu: D(d)u – black. SN 7927.

Craig Derlwyn: At the oak grove. SN 7215.

Craig Fan Las: At the blue peak. SO 0519.

Craig Gwaun Taf: In the marsh by the river Taf. SO 0020.

Craig Pwllfa: By the pool side. SO 0620.

Craig Syddi: Syddi may derive from

Cribyn

syddyn, an old Welsh word for a dwelling. SO 2910.

Craig y Byllfa: *Poolside rock.* SO 0019.

Craig y Castell: By the castle. SO 1716.

Craig y Cilau: *Rock of refuge.* A National Nature Reserve established in 1959. SO 1816.

Craig y Fan Ddu: By the dark summit. SO 0518.

Craig y Fan: At the summit. SO 0719.

Craig y Fro: *The vale crag.* SN 9620.

Craig y nos: Nos: night. A gothic folly built here in c 1842 associated with the opera singer Adelina Patti, who bought it in 1878. SN 8315.

Craig y Rhiwarth: At the ridge hill. The site of a prehistoric hillfort and the Brecknock Wildlife Trust Nature Reserve. SN 8415.

Craig y Sawrwg: In the scented place. SN 7619.

Craig yr Allt: On the wooded hill slope. SO 2906.

Craig yr hafod: By the summer dwelling. SO 2710.

Cribarth: The crest of the hillside. SN 8314.

Cribyn Du: *Little black crest.* SN 7324.

Cribyn: *Ridge of hill or little crest.* Cribyn can also mean an outcrop of rock on high land. SO 0221.

Crochan Sion Hopkyn: Sion Hopkyn's well. SO 1616.

Cronfa: *reservoir*

Cronfa Ddŵr Cantref: *Cantref Reservoir.* The middle of the three reservoirs in the Taf Fawr Valley. Completed in 1892. The farms Glan crew, Crewisaf, Abercrew and Blaentaf were demolished in order to construct the reservoir. SN 9915.

Cronfa Ddŵr Crai: *Crai Reservoir.* Built in 1898 – 1906 by Swansea Corporation to supply water to the Swansea area. SN 8821.

Cronfa Ddŵr Llwyn Onn: *Llwyn Onn Reservoir.* The southernmost of the three reservoirs. It was completed in 1926. The hamlet of Ynysyfelin (*The river meadow of the mill*) was flooded in 1914 in order to build the reservoir. Farms and smallholdings, the village school, two public houses and Bethel Welsh Baptist Chapel built in 1799 and Melin y pwllcoch (*Redpond Mill*) were all lost. It is known that Melin y pwllcoch was a corn mill in 1651 and later converted to a woollen

Crughywel Castle

factory which was closed in 1891/1895. The Baptist chapel of Bethel was rebuilt in 1914 at the village of Llwyn Onn, the opposite side to the reservoir. SO 0012.

Cronfa Ddŵr Nant moel: Nantmoel translates as *bare valley*. SN 9807.

Cronfa Ddŵr Penderyn: Penderyn translates as *bird's head*. The reservoir was completed in 1920. SN 9307.

Cronfa Ddŵr Pentwyn: Pentwyn means *head of the dune*. The reservoir was built by the Merthyr Tydfil Local Board of Health by an Act of Parliament in 1858 following outbreaks of cholera in Merthyr Tydfil and in parts of south Wales. It was also known as Dolygaer lake. The reservoir is now incorporated into the Pontsticill Reservoir following leakage problems. SO 0514.

Cronfa Ddŵr Ponsticill: Pontsticill means *stile bridge*. The reservoir was completed in 1927 when 8 farms and some cottages together with Capel Taf Fechan, Capel Bethlehem and Dolygaer Church were drowned by the construction. SO 0513.

Cronfa Ddŵr Talybont: Talybont means *bridge at brow of hill*. SO 0918.

Cronfa Ddŵr Wysg: Wysg is derived from the Latin word 'isca' which meant fish. It is believed the headquarters of the Roman Second Legion, 'Isca Augusta' was the fort 'Gobannio' in Abergavenny on the banks of the Usk and this is how the name of the river originated. (Usk). SN 8228.

Cronfa Ddŵr y Bannau: *Beacons Reservoir*. The northernmost of the reservoirs in the Brecon Beacons, completed in 1897. SN 9818.

Cronfa Ddŵr Ystradfellte: Ystradfellte means vale of *river Mellte – lightening/fast-flowing river*. SN 9417.

Crucornau Fawr: *Peaked mounds*. (Crucorney). SO 3024.

Crughywel: *Hywel's mound*. The remains of a 13th century castle can be found near the centre of the town. It was taken by Edward 11 in 1322 and defended against Owain Glyndwr in 1403. George Everest, (1790 – 1866) the acclaimed surveyor and Surveyor General of India was born in Gwernvale Crughywel. He had the distinction of the world's highest mountain being named after him. (Crickhowell) SO 2118.

Near Cribyn Summit

Cwar: *quarry*

Cwar Blaen Dyffryn: Upper vale. Disused quarry. SO 1014.

Cwar Du Mawr: Big shaded. SN 8021.

Cwar Llwyd: Grey. A small disused quarry. SN 9717.

Cwar Pen y porth: At the head of the entrance. SN 9312.

Cwar Penrhiw wen: At the top of the white hill. SN 7317.

Cwar y Gigfran: Raven. SO 0619.

Cwar yr Hendre: The winter-dwelling. Disused limestone quarry workings. SO 0914.

Cwar yr Ystrad: Valley or vale. Ystrad can also refer to a wide valley bottom. The site of a large quarry. A medieval Ogham stone inscribed in Irish script, can be found at Cwar yr Ystrad. SO 0814.

Cwm: *narrow, deep valley*

Cwm Banw: Banw is an old Welsh word for young deer or pig. SO 2223.

Cwm Bont-gam: Curved bridge. SN 8034.

Cwm Brychan: *Brychan's valley.* SO 2532.

Cwm Bwcher: Bwcher may derive from bwch which means a buck in Welsh. SO 2827.

Cwm Cadlan: Battlefield ridge. Site of Bronze Age cairn. See entry for Cefn Cadlan. SN 9609.

Cwm Callan: Callan is the name of the stream. SO 0614.

Cwm Camlais: Of the winding stream. Site of the remains of a small castle destroyed in 1265. It may have been built by Llywelyn ap Gruffudd. The castle was known in previous times as Camlais, Maescar, Blaencamlais or Defynoch Castle. SN 9528.

Cwm Canol: Middle. SN 8013.

Cwm Carneilw: Second cairn. SO 1513.

Cwm Claisfer: Little stream valley or slow flowing narrow stream. A valley in the Parish of Llangynidr. Cwm Cleisfer is also a Brecknock Wildlife Nature Resreve. SO 1416.

Cwm Clyd: Sheltered. SN 7830; SO 2230.

Cwm Clydach: *Clydach vale.* See entry for Clydach. Cwm Clydach is a RSPB Nature Reserve. SO 2012.

Cwm Coed-y-cerrig: Wood of the stones. A National Nature Reserve. SO 2921.

Cwm Crai: *Crai valley.* See entry for Crai. SN 8927.

Cwm Crew: Of the clamorous stream – a waterfall. See entry for Cefn Crew. SO 0018.

Cwm Sorgwn

Cwm Criban: Little crest. Criban may be a corruption of cribyn. SO 0713.

Cwm Cwareli: Quarries. SO 0521.

Cwm Cwta: Short. SN 8426.

Cwm Cwy: Cwy features in the name of a small stream, Nant Cwy. SO 0922.

Cwm Cynwyn: *Head of white valley*. In this area is the site of the remains of stone enclosures called, 'Hafodydd', which were used for containing sheep moved to these higher pastures during spring. SO 0322.

Cwm Du: Dark. (Llanfihangel Cwm Du: *St Michael's Church in the dark valley*, is the older name for Cwm Du). Thomas Price (Carnhuanwc) is buried here in his parish. The Nant y Ffin tavern in Llanfihangel Cwm Du is a Grade II listed building which was originally a drovers inn. SO 1823

Cwm Ddeunant: Of the two streams. SO 2526.

Cwm Dringarth: Of the sloping hill. SN 9417.

Cwm Du Ysfa: *Dark valley of the sheep drive*. SN 8431.

Cwm Dŵr y coed: Of the wood stream. SO 1932.

Cwm Dyar: Noisy. SO 2312.

Cwm Dyry: Wild. SO 0011.

Cwm Ffos Ddu: Black dyke. SN 8129.

Cwm Ffrwd: Of the fast-flowing stream. SO 0107; SO 2723.

Cwm Gelanedd: Of the slaughter. Site of Roman camps and battle grounds. SO 1124.

Cwm Gelli Gam: Crooked groves. SN 8429.

Cwm Goetre: Of the settlement by the wood. SN 7427.

Cwm Golau: Bright. SN 8034.

Cwm Gored: Open or fish-trap. SN 9008.

Cwm Gors: Of the marsh. SN 8426.

Cwm Grigws Uchaf: *Upper Grigws valley*. Grigws has been described as an ancient residence of kings of Brycheiniog. SO 2230.

Cwm Gwenffrwd: White stream. SO 2517.

Cwm Gwernfelin: Alder mill. SN 7932.

Cwm Haffes: Valley of drought. SN 8317.

Cwm Henwen: Old white. SN 8329.

Cwm Hydfer: Short stretch. SN 8526.

Cwm Iou: *yoke-shaped valley*. St Martin's Church in Cwmiou dates back to the Middle Ages and contains a medieval cross described as one of the crosses of the Pilgrims' Way to St David's. (Cwmyoy). SO 3023.

Cwm Llwch: Of the lake. SO 0023.

Cwm Llwyfog: Elms territory. SN 8332.

Cwm Iou church

Cwm Llwyn-cor: Little grove. SN 8628.

Cwm Llwyn-Meurig: Meurig's grove. SN 8528.

Cwm Llwyn-y-bedw: The birch grove. SN 7326.

Cwm Llysiog: Llysiog may be derive from llysieuog which means herbal. SO 0114.

Cwm Meity: Middle house. SN 8525.

Cwm Moel: Moel – bare. SO 0311.

Cwm Mydan: Mydan may be the St. Medan buried at Bodmin, Cornwall. He was the son of Pasgen ab Urien, King of Gwyr in c522. SN 7832.

Cwm Nant-cil-y-clawdd: At the boundary retreat stream. SN 8427.

Cwm Nant Ddu: Of the black stream. SN 8923.

Cwm Nant dywyll: Of the dark stream. SN 7319.

Cwm Nant Hir: Of the long stream. SN 9807.

Cwm Nant Lloi: Calves stream. SN 8618.

Cwm Nant yr Ychen: The oxen stream. SO 1826.

Cwm Nant: Of the stream. SN 9314.

Cwm Nant-gam: Of the winding stream. SO 2112.

Cwm Nantybeudy: Of the cowshed stream. SN 8030.

Cwm Nant-y-Fedw: Of the birch-grove stream. SO 2026.

Cwm Nantygarreg: Of the rock stream. SO 1924.

Cwm Nantypistyll: Of the waterfall stream. SN 8728.

Cwm Newynydd: Famine land. SN 7626; SN 8622.

Cwm Oergwm: *Cold valley.* Cwm Oergwm is a Brecknock Wildlife Trust Nature Reserve. SO 0623.

Cwm Onnau: Onnau – ash. SO 1817.

Cwm Pantlladron: Of the thieves hollow. SO 1616.

Cwm Pedol: Of the horseshoe. SN 7016.

Cwm Porth: *Gateway valley.* SN 9312.

Cwm Pwllharri: At Harri's pool or pit. SN 8033.

Cwm Pyrgad: Pyr is an old obscure word in Welsh meaning lords and cad can mean a battle. SO 1015.

Cwm Rhiw calch: Lime hill SN 8232.

Cwm Rhiwlas: Green hill. SN 8332.

Cwm Rhyd Ellyw: *Valley at the ford of Ellyw.* Ellyw was a daughter of Brychan the 5th century ruler of Brycheiniog. SO 1734.

Cwm Sawdde Fechan: *Valley of the little Sawdde river.* See entry for Afon Sawdde. SN 7620.

Sgŵd Gwladys on Pyrddin river

Cwm Sere: Sere may be a personal name. SO 0223.

Cwm Siencyn: The name of the brook. (Cwm Shenkyn). SO 1525.

Cwm Sorgwn: *Sorgwn valley.* SO 1726.

Cwm Sychnant: *Parched valley.* SO 0515.

Cwm Taf Fechan: *Valley of the little river Taf.* SO 0510.

Cwm Taf: *Taf Valley.* Woodland area of Special Scientific Interest and a Local Nature Reserve. SO 0110.

Cwm Taldrum: Tall ridge. SN 7626.

Cwm tan y mynydd: Below the mountain. SN 8231.

Cwm Treddfin: Treddfin may derive from trefddyn, an old word in Welsh for home. SN 8431.

Cwm Treweryn: Of the settlement by the alders. SN 9126.

Cwm Trosnant: Scattered stream or over the brook. SO 2717.

Cwm Tŷ-hen: Old house. SN 7730.

Cwm Tynewydd: New house. SN 7729.

Cwm y Cadno: The fox. Site of Roman Practice Works – a small Roman camp. SN 8130.

Cwm y Gorlan: The sheep fold. SO 0614.

Cwm y Gribin: Gribin or cribin may be a local spelling of cribyn which means little crest/rake. SN 8031.

Cwm y Meirch: Of the stallions. SN 8232.

Cwm y Nant: The brook. SO 1931.

Cwm yr Afon: The river. SN 8324.

Cwm yr Hom: *The Hom valley.* SO 2427.

Cwm yr Olchfa: Of the washing-place. SN 8030.

Cwmgwdi: Of the twisting stream. Gwdi was the old name of a local stream – Nant gwdi. SO 0225.

Cwmwysg: *Wysg valley.* See entry for Afon Wysg. (Usk valley). SN 8528.

Cwterydd Blaen Twrch Fechan: *Channels at the source of the little boar river.* SN 7820.

Cylchau: *Circles.* SN 7520.

Sgŵd Einion Gam and Sgŵd Uchaf Clun-gwyn in Cwm Nedd

Dan: *under/below*

Dan y Darren: The crag or craggy hill. Former limestone quarry and a wildlife site. SO 1916.

Dan yr Ogof: The cave. The National Showcaves Centre for Wales. Bronze Age people lived and buried their dead in the caves. SN 8315.

Danywenallt: *Under milk wood.* YHA hostel and study centre. SO 1020.

Dardy: *Dark oak-tree.* Dar may derive from dâr which means oak-tree. SO 2018.

Darren: *ridge/escarpment/outcrop*

Darren Cilau: Retreats. SO 2015.

Darren Clôg Fawr: Great cliff. SO 1116.

Darren Ddu: Black outcrop/black rock. SO 1015.

Darren Fach: Little. SO 0816.

Darren Fawr: Large. Brecknock Wildlife Nature Reserve. SO 0816.

Darren Lwyd: Grey. SO 2333.

Defynnog: *Land of Dyfwn, a personal name.* Gwenllian Morgan (1852 – 1939) was born at Defynnog. Gwenllian Morgan was the first woman to become a mayor in Brecon. SN 9227.

Deri: *Oak woodland.* SO 2917.

Derlwyn Isaf: *Lower oak grove.* SN 7614.

Disgwylfa: *Look-out mountain.* SN 8117; SN 8123.

Dolygaer: *Meadow by the fort.* Dol usually means a meadow near a river bank. Outdoor Education Centre. SO 0614.

Dorwen ar Gïedd: *Hillside on the river Cïedd.* See afon Gïedd. SN 8115.

Drysgol: *Rough mountain.* SN 6815.

Dunant: *Black brook.* SN 7925.

Dŵr Llydan: *Wide water.* SN 8327.

Dyffryn Crawnon: *Valley of the Crawnon river, place of wild garlic.* See afon Crawnon. SO 1218.

Dyffryn Ewias: *Vale of Ewias.* Named after Cantref Ewias. The location of the medieval priory of Llanthony. (Vale of Ewyas) SO 2728.

Dyffryn Nedd: Nedd derives from nida, a Brythoneg or old Welsh word for shining stream or river. SN 9112.

Dyfnant: *Deep stream.* SN 7825.

Dyfnant Wysg: *Fast stream of the Wysg.* SN 8126.

Dyffryn Ewias – Vale of Ewias

Eglwys Faen: *Stone church.* The name of a cave in Llangatwg. SO 1915.

Esgair Ddu: *Black ridge.* SN 7820.

Esgair Hir: *Long ridge.* SN 7719.

Faenor: *Place of the Maenor – administrative unit.* Eglwys y Faenor: *Vaynor Church*, was originally built of wood in AD 874. It was dedicated to St. Gwynno, a sixth century saint, who is also the patron saint of Llanwynno and one of the three saints of Llantrisant: *Church of three saints*. St. Gwynno's Church, Vaynor was destroyed by fire during the battle of Maes y Faenor in c 1290. The church was rebuilt of stone in 1295 and the tower still stands today. It fell into decay during the latter half of the 19th century and the present church was built in 1870 and financed by Robert Thomson Crawshay. He was the ironmaster of Cyfarthfa Castle in Merthyr Tydfil. He died in 1879 and his grave is to be found in Vaynor Churchyard. His body is buried beneath a heavy stone slab bearing the inscription 'God Forgive Me'. (Vaynor). SO 0410.

Fagl Bengam: *Crooked head stream or stone.* SN 7920.

Fan: *summit/peak/high mountain*

Fan Brycheiniog: Of Brycheiniog. The highest peak, 802 metres, of the Black Mountain. SN 8221.

Fan Frynach and Craig Cerrig-gleisiad

Fan Dringarth: Of the sloping hill. SN 9419.

Fan Fawr: Great. SN 9619.

Fan Fechan: Little. SN 8319.

Fan Fraith: Speckled. SN 8818.

Fan Frynach: *Brynach's summit/mountain.* Brynach was a 5th/6th century saint of Irish origin. A trig point is found on the peak and Fan Frynach is a designated National Nature Reserve. SN 9522.

Fan Gyhirych: Ridged. SN 8819.

Fan Hir: Long. SN 8319.

Fan Llia: Llia is a personal name and the name of a stream. The prehistoric stone 'Maen Llia' stands near the stream's source. SN 9318.

Fan Nedd: By the river Nedd. Nedd derives from the Brythoneg 'nida' which means shining stream. SN 1891.

Fan y Big: Tapered. SO 0320.

Fan-Foel: Bare. Site of Bronze Age burial mound. SN 8222.

Fedw Fawr: *Great birchgrove.* SN 8027.

Felin Crai: *Mill on the river Crai.* See entry for Crai. Felin Crai was originally the site of a corn mill. SN 8823.

Felindre: *Mill settlement.* SO 1723.

Felindre: *Mill settlement or hamlet.* Felindre was once a hamlet of several cottages including 'Trefedw' or 'Tre Bedw', *Birch homestead*, now demolished. In his History of Brecknockshire, Theophilus Jones claims the mill was built in the 15th century. This was during the reign of Humphrey Stafford, the Duke of Buckingham and the lord of Brecon, who was described as an 'implacable tyrant', who subjected his tenants to unfair taxes and sought to secure their land at every opportunity. Evan ap Phillip Howel of Llanfrynach resisted and refused to pay homage to the Duke and when he was arrested and imprisoned in the goal in Gloucester for three years, his wife built the mill on his estate 'Felin Fach', which became the hamlet of Felindre. SO 0626.

Fenni Fach: *The lesser river by the smithies.* Coed Fenni Fach is the site of an Iron Age hillfort. SO 0228.

Ffald Dolau Haffes: *Sheepfold meadow at the river Haffes.* See entry for river Haffes. SN 8218.

Ffald Newydd: *New sheepfold.* Site of cairns. SN 9714.

Ffald Newydd: *New sheepfold.* SO 0219.

Ffald Truman: *Truman's sheepfold.* SN 7420.

Ffawyddog: *Place of beech trees.* SO 2018.

Ffinant: *Boundary stream.* SN 7225.

Fforch Ceulan: *Fork at river bank.* SN 7519.

Fforchaman: *Fork on river Aman.* See Afon Aman. SN 7415.

Ffordd las fawr: *Great green way.* SO 2623.

Ffordd Las/Bwlch Main: *Green road/thin gap.* SO 0622.

Ffordd Las: *Green road.* SO 2038.

Fforest Fawr: *Great forest.* The Fforest Fawr Geopark is an area in the Brecon Beacons National Park, a designated area of geological significance. SN 8819.

Ffos y Wern: *Ditch at the alder-grove.* SO 1014.

Ffrwd Ganol fach: *Little middle stream.* SO 0208.

Ffrwd Ganol fawr: *Great middle stream.* SO 0207.

Ffrwd Las: *Blue stream.* SN 7716.

Ffrwd y Felin: *The mill stream.* SN 7024.

Ffrwdgrech: *Rippling stream.* Ffrwd can describe a torrent and also a lesser brook. SO 0327.

Ffrydiau Twrch: *Streams at the river Twrch.* See Afon Twrch. SN 7716.

Ffynnon Bryn-bach: *Little hill spring.* SN 9017.

Ffawyddog, Grwyne Fawr

Ffynnon: *well/spring*

Ffynnon Cae Rhos: In the field on the moor. SO 1316.

Ffynnon Ddu: Black. SN 8415.

Ffynnon Ddu (ogof): *The cave of the black well.* SN 9208.

Ffynnon Dwym Hirgan: Long white warm. SO 1616.

Ffynnon Garreg Fawr: Great rock. SN 9313.

Ffynnon Lysiog: Llysiog may derive from llysieuog which can mean herbal. SO 0215.

Ffynnon Oer: Cold. SO 1525; SO 1923.

Ffynnon Tâl y pyst: At the top of the posts. SO 1517.

Ffynnon Tŷ berth: At the house in the copse. SO 1718.

Ffynnon Tyle-brith: At the speckled hill. SN 9917.

Ffynnon y Brain: The crows. SO 1617.

Ffynnon y Ddraenen: The thorn. SO 1616.

Ffynnon y Gwyddau: Of the geese. SN 8524.

Ffynnon y Wern: The alder-grove. SN 7730.

Foel: *bare hill-top*

Foel Darw: The bull. SN 8225.

Ffynnon Isio, holy well at Patrisio

Foel Deg: Fair. SN 7315.

Foel Deg ar bedol: On the horseshoe path. Site of cairns and an old drovers route. SN 7015.

Foel Fawr: Great. SN 7318.

Foel Fraith: The mottle. 7518.

Fron Uchaf: *The highest rounded hill.* SN 8032.

Gadair Fawr: *The great mountain ridge.* Cadair can mean a mountain ridge in the shape of a seat. SO 2228.

Gaer/Twyn y Gaer: *Hill of the fort.* Site of an Iron Age hill-fort. SO 2921.

Gallt y Fron: *Wooded hillside.* SN 7733.

Garn Ddu: *Black cairn.* Site of a menhir – a standing stone. Area of disused limekilns. SN 9511.

Garn Ddu: *Black cairn.* SO 0212.

Garn Ddyrys: *Wild cairn.* SO 2611.

Garn Fach: *Little cairn.* SO 1116.

Garn Fawr: *Great cairn.* SN 7822.

Garn Fawr: *Great cairn.* SO 1215.

Garn Ganol: *Middle cairn.* SN 9514.

Garn Lâs: *Blue cairn.* SN 8224.

Garreg Fawr: *Great rock.* SN 8214.

Garreg Las: *Blue rock.* Bronze age cairns, known as Carnau'r Garreg Las are found on the summit. 7720.

Garreg Lwyd: *Grey rock.* Otherwise known as Moel Gornach: *bare peak.* SN 9412.

Garwnant Fach: *Little coarse stream.* SN 9912.

Garwnant Fawr: *Great coarse stream.* SN 9913.

Garwnant: *Coarse stream.* Forestry Commission Wales Visitor Centre. SO 0013.

Gellifelen: *Yellow copse.* SO 2112.

Gelli Gandryll Y: *Fragmented copse.* The imposing castle overlooking the town had a chequered history. It was built by the Normans in the 11/12th century and seized and burnt together with the town by King John in the early 13th century and later rebuilt by Reginald Braose. Llywelyn ap Iorwerth attacked the castle and burnt the town in 1231. The castle later became the base for Henry 111's conflict with rebel Norman lords including Walter Clifford and Its occupancy changed until it was seized by the English Crown in 1322. The castle was later besieged by Owain Glyndwr in 1402. The English name Hay derives from an old English word, '(g) haeg' which meant an enclosed area of a forest for the purpose of hunting. (Hay). SO 2242.

Gïedd Fach: *Little raging stream.* SN 8220.

Gilwern: *Shelter of the alder trees.* SO 2414.

Gist Wen: *White coffin.* SO 0621.

Glangrwyne: see Llangrwyne. SO. 2416.

Glanwysg: *Bank of the river Usk.* SO 2315.

Glanusk: glanwysg – *bank of the river Usk.* SO 1919.

Glanyscir: *Bank of the river Ysgir – ysgir has been translated as meaning 'ittle blade'.* SO 0030.

Glastir y Picws: *Green land of the Picws mountain – picws may refer to a peak – Picws Du is a peak of the Black Mountain in Carmarthenshire.* SN 8021.

Gloddfa Ddu: *Black quarry or mine.* SO 0418.

Glog Las: *Green crag.* Site of a round cairn. SN 9514.

Glyn Collwn: *Hazel grove or valley.* Collwn may derive from collwyn which means hazel grove. Roland Mathias, the writer and poet, was born in 1915 at Ffynnon Fawr a farmhouse in Glyn Collwn. SO 0817.

Glyn Llydan: *Wide valley.* SN 6819.

Glyn Tarell: *Bank or valley of the river Tarell.* See afon Tarell. SN 9723.

Glyn Tawe: *Vale of river Tawe.* SN 8416.

Glyn wyrdd: *Green valley.* SN 7021.

Round cairn on Garn Fawr

Godre'r foel darw: *Treeless bottom of the 'darw' – bull.* Tarw may derive from tarw which means bull in Welsh. SN 8126.

Godre'r Garn Las: *Bottom of the blue cairn.* SN 8125.

Godre'r Garreg Las: *Bottom of the blue rock.* SN 7719.

Goetre Wharf: *Woodland dwelling at the wharf.* The location of a 200 year old industrial heritage site on the Monmouthshire to Brecon canal. SO 3106.

Gorlan Tyn-y-waun: *Fold of the small farm at the mountain pasture.* SO 0417.

Gorlan yr Allt: *Sheepfold hill.* SO 0515.

Gorllwm: May describe an open exposed area. SN 9621.

Gofilon: *The forge.* Gofilon probably derives from 'gefail' which is the Welsh word for forge. SO 2613. (Govilon).

Graig Fan Ddu: *Black peak rock.* SO 0018.

Graig: *The rock.* SO 2516.

Graig Fraith: *Mottled rock.* SN 7117.

Grwyne Fawr: *Greater Grwyne river.* Grwyne refers to a river through ridged land. The location of the Grwyne reservoir and where the river flows into the river Usk. SO 2230.

Grwyne Fechan: *The lesser Grwyne river.* SO 2422.

Gwal y Cadno: *The foxes lair.* SN 8222.

Gwalciau'r Cwm: *The valley ridge.* SO 0619.

Gwaun: *moor*

Gwaun Bryn-bwch: Buck hill. SN 9111.

Gwaun Cefn y garreg: Of the ridge of the rock. SN 9413.

Gwaun Cerrig Llwydion: Of the grey stones. Site of a nearby cairn. It is described as a peat covered area, known as 'moon country' because of the geography of the area. Gwaun can also represent a wet or boggy area. SO 0419.

Gwaun Crew: At the clamorous stream. SN 9917.

Gwaun Danydarren: Below the crag or craggy hill. Darren can also refer to rocky or barren land. SO 0815.

Gwaun goch dimau: Round, red. SN 9109.

Gwaun Hepste: At river Hepste – see Afon Hepste. SN 9312.

Gwaun Nant Ddu: Black/dark stream. SO 0017; SO 0815.

Gwaun Perfedd: Middle/central. SO 0220.

Gwaun Taf: *Taf moor.* SO 0119.

Gwaun y Ffa: The beans. SO 1813.

Gwaun y Pynt: Pynt may derive from epynt, a place or track where horses or ponies roam. See Mynydd Epynt. SO 0315.

Gwegil y Picws: *Nape of the peak.* SN 8121.
Gwely Ifan y Rhiw: *The resting-place of Ifan of the hill.* SN 8222.
Gwern Picoed: *Alder-trees at magpie wood.* SN 9011.
Gweunydd Hepste: *Meadows at afon Hepste.* See afon Hepste. SN 9412.
Gwys Fach: *Lesser gwys stream.* Gwys may derive from gwŷs which is an obscure word in Welsh for pig. SN 7815.

Hay Bluff: Penybegwn in Welsh. Begwn or begwns, an obscure name, said to be a corruption of 'Beacons'. SO 2436
Held Wood: *Wood or holding.* Held is an old English word for 'slope', which occurs in the Border Counties often as a wood held with the manor. Hence the 'Held wood' between Cantref and Ffrwdgrech. Held is also said to be a translation of the Welsh word gafael which meant a share of land inherited by sons from their father's land. SO 0327.
Helgwm: *Hunters wood or hunter's valley.* SN 6720.
Hen Allt Common: *The old wood common.* Site of scientific interest. SO 2339.
Heol Beili Glas: *Green yard way.* SN 7831.
Heol Cae du: *Black field way.* SN 7731.

Heol Lân: *Holy or sacred way.* SN ?
Heol Llidiart coch: *Red gate lane.* SN 7121.
Heol Llwyn moch: *Pigs grove road.* SN 7724.
Heol Senni: *Road by river Senni.* Senni may derive from the personal name Sannan and refer to saint Sannan who was an Irish monk in the 6th century. SN 9223.
Heol y Cartws: *Cart-house way.* SN 7322.
Heol y Gelli: *The groves road.* SN 7421.

Libanus: *Lebanon, the biblical name.* The local chapel of Libanus, originally built in 1823 gave its name to the village. SN 9925.

Llan: *church/parish centre*
Llanbedr: Saint Pedr or Peter's church. Llan originally referred to a house or building enclosed by a defensive hedge or wall. It more commonly appears before the name of a saint as the name of a church and a parish or village. It is also known as, Llanbedr Ystrad Yw: *Saint Peter's church in the valley of the yews.* SO 2320.
Llanbrynean: *Hillhouse.* A 19th century house built by David Morgan, 1833 – 1919, the founder of the David Morgan Store in

Hay Bluff

Cardiff. Born in Brecon, David Morgan became an apprentice draper in Newport at the age of 14. He moved to Cardiff, aged 46, acquired properties in the Hayes and founded 'David Morgans', which became the second largest department store in Cardiff. The store was closed in 2005. SO 0725

Llanddeusant: *Of the two saints (Simon and Jude).* SN 7724.

Llanddewi Nant Hodni: *Of Dewi Sant by the Nant Hodni (the placid stream).* The ruins of Llanthony Abbey, built by Augustian monks in the 12th century, is located here. (Llanthony) SO 2827.

Llanddewi Ysgryd: *Of Dewi Sant/St. David on the rocky mountain.* (Llanddewi Skirrid) SO 3417.

Llandeilo Bertholau: *Of saint Teilo of the sullied porch.* SO 3116.

Llanelli: *Of saint Elli.* Elli may derive from Ellyw, who was a daughter of Brychan Brycheiniog in the 6th century. SO 2314.

Llanfaes: *In the open field.* SO 0328.

Llanfihangel Crucornau: *Of saint Michael by the peaked mounds.* SO 3220.

Llanfrynach: *Of Saint Brynach.* The church is dedicated to the 5/6th century Celtic saint of Irish origin. The church stands in the middle of the village in one of the largest churchyards in the county. The oldest part of the church is the tower which was said to have been built by the Normans in about 1201 as some kind of fortification. The church buildings deteriorated by the turn of the 18th century and the church of Saint Brynach was rebuilt between 1855 and 1856 and it was officially opened by the Bishop of St. David's on the 13th May 1856. SO 0725.

Llangasty Tal-y-llyn: *Of saint Gastayn at the head of the lake (Syfaddan or Llangors).* St. Gastayn was a 5th century saint, who was reputedly the tutor of st. Cynog. SO 1326.

Llangatwg: *Of Saint Cadog.* Cadog or Catwg was a 5/6th century saint, the son of Gwladys, who was one of the many daughters of Brychan Brycheiniog. One of the longest cave systems in Britain lies beneath Mynydd Llangatwg. The three main caves are; Ogof Agen Allwedd: *Key crevice cave*, Ogaf Darren Cilau: *Rock Recesses Cave*, Ogaf Craig a Ffynnon: *Fountain Rock Cave.* (Llangattock). SO 2117.

Llangenau, Llangenni: *Of Saint Ceneu* a daughter of Brychan Brycheiniog. SO 2417.

Llanddewi Nant Hodni

Llangors: *At the place of reeds or marsh.* Llangors lake is otherwise known as Llyn Syfaddan. Llangors was the ancient capital of Brycheiniog. An ancient crannog – a lake dwelling, can be found on the lake, which has been restored to its original glory. SO 1327.

Llangrwyne: *By the river Crwyne.* SO 2416.

Llangynidr: *Of Saint Cynidr, a 6th century saint and the son of Ceingar, who was a daughter of Brychan Brycheiniog.* The remains of a Norman castle at Blaenllynfi (SO 145 229), built in the early 13th century was seized by Llywelyn ap Gruffudd in 1262. It deteriorated by the reign of Edward 11 in the early 14th century. The six-arch bridge (c.1600) which spans the Usk, is one of the finest of its type. Ogof Fawr: *Great cave*, which is also known as the 'Chartists' cave', is found at Mynydd Llangynidr. SO 1519.

Llanhamlach: *On the other side of the lake or church of Anlach.* The latter is probably a less plausible translation referring to Anlach son of Coronoc and father of Brychan Brycheiniog. Anlach is reputedly buried before the porch at the church of Llansbyddid. The church in Llanhamlach is one of 19 churches or parishes in Wales dedicated to St. Illtud. A prehistoric tomb called Tŷ Illtud stands on a hill above the church and was reputedly used as a hermitage by Illtud. The chamber is covered by a capstone and is aligned towards Pen y Fan and is a protected archaeological site. Ffynnon Illtud nearby is the name of the stream which flows between the parishes of Llanhamlach and Llansantffraed. A menhir or maen-hir – a long stone or standing stone can be found near the site of Tŷ Illtud. It is one of eight territorial or guiding marker stones to be found along the river Usk between Brecon and Gilwern. SO 0926.

Llanigon, Llaneigion: *Of St. Eigon, who was a brother of St. Cynidr and Cadog – see Llangynidr and Llangadog.* Neolithic tombs are found in the area. The place was also known for its Nonconformist activity in the 17th century. A school was established at Llwynllwyd by David Price, where Howel Harris and Williams Williams Pantycelyn were pupils. SO 2139.

Llannerch goch: Red glade. SN 8131.

Llansanffraid: *Of St. Ffraid (Brigid).* The author, physician and poet Henry Vaughan 1622 – 1695 was born in Llansantffraid and he is buried at Llansanffraid Church. SO 1223.

Llanspyddid: *Church by the hawthorn trees.* The church is dedicated to St. Cadog, who reputedly built a monastery here. SO 0128.

Llanwenarth: *Church of Saint Gwenarth.* SO 2714.

Llech Llia: *Llia's stone.* See afon Llia. The site of a Bronze Age circular earthwork enclosure. SN 9219.

Llethr y Llyn: *Slope at the lake.* SN 8022.

Llethr: *The incline.* SN 9119.

Llorfa: *Place of the column.* The site of an early Bronze Age stone circle. SN 7815.

Llwyncwmstabl: *Stable valley grove.* Site of a prehistoric round cairn. SN 7715.

Llwyn Onn: *Ash grove.* The name of the hamlet and of the southernmost of the three reservoirs in the Taf Fawr valley. The hamlet of Ynysyfelin (*The river meadow of the mill*) was flooded in 1914 to build the reservoir. Farms and smallholdings, the village school, two public houses and Bethel Baptist Chapel built in 1799, as well as the local mill, Melin y pwllcoch (*Redpond mill*) were all lost with drowning of the valley. Bethel chapel was later rebuilt in 1914/15 on the opposite side to the reservoir at the village of Llwyn Onn. SO 0111.

Llwyn-Onn reservoir

Llygad Hepste-fechan: *Eye/spring of the little Hepste stream.* See afon Hepste. The site of Bronze Age hut circles, enclosures and cairns. SN 9614.

Llyn: *lake*

Llyn Bach: Little. SN 9312.

Llyn Cwm Llwch: In the Llwch valley. (Llwch is an old Welsh word for lake.) It has also been called, Pwll y Doctor: *The Doctor's Pond*, named after a well known scholar, Dr. David John Rhys, who lived in an old farmhouse down the valley. According to legend an enchanted island appeared in the middle of the lake on May Day with a display of fairy flowers which could be gathered to fairy music. However, a foolhardy visitor picked some flowers and the island disappeared forever. SO 0022.

Llyn Du Isaf: Lower black. SN 6918.

Llyn Du Uchaf: Higher black. SN 7018.

Llyn Fignenfelen: At the yellow-top peak. SN 7118.

Llyn Llywarch: Llywarch may refer to the 9th/10th century Welsh bard, who reputedly composed the poem Canu *Llywarch Hen* at Llangors crannog. SN 9616.

Llyn Mawr: Great. SN 9312.

Llyn Pen-fathor: Mathor may be personal name. Pen Fathor Uchaf is the name of a nearby cairn. SN 9515.

Llyn Syfaddan: *Syfaddan's lake (person's name)*. See Llangors. SO 1326.

Llyn Traeth-bach: Little, by the shingle shore. SN 8725.

Llyn y Fan Fach: By the little summit. The lake is associated with the legend of the Lady of the Lake. A local man married a beautiful girl who arose from the lake, they prospered and produced three sons. However, he breached the condition of the marriage by inadvertently hitting her three times and she returned to the lake forever. The three sons went on to become the famous doctors known as the Physicians of Myddfai. SN 8021.

Llyn y Fan Fawr: By the big summit. The summit is Fan Brycheiniog, the highest peak in the Black Mountain. SN 8321.

Llyngeren: Ceren may be personal name. SO 0512.

Llynnant: In the stream. SN 6921.

Llynnau'r Waun: *The meadow lakes.* SN 9515.

Llywel: *Church of Llywel.* It is described as the church of the three saints, Dewi, Teilo and Llywel. Llywel was reputedly a disciple of Dyfrig and Teilo in the 6th century. SN 8730.

Login: *See Corn Du.* SO 0024.

Maen Llia: *Llia's stone.* An ancient menhir or standing stone. SN 9219.

Maen Llwyd: *Grey or sacred stone.* A standing stone. SO 2227.

Maen Madog: *Madog's stone.* A standing stone near the Roman road, Sarn Helen. The stone has a Latin inscription, 'DERVACUS FILIUS JUSTI IC JACIT', which translates as, 'Dervacus, son of Justus, lies here.' Dervacus was a Roman name in the 6th century. SN 9115.

Maen Mawr: *Great stone.* A large standing stone. SN 8420.

Maes y Faenor: *Maenor field or* **Cae Burydd:** *Field of the lords (Norman)*. It has also been called 'The field of slaughter'. It was the site of a famous battle in 1290 between Gilbert de Clare, Lord of Glamorgan and Humphrey de Bohun, Lord of Brecknock. The mound on Cae Burydd was excavated in 1823 in the presence of the Reverend Thomas Price (Carnhuanwc), the Vicar of Cwmdu, and many human bones were found as well as

Llyn Cwm Llwch from Corn Du

the remains of iron weapons. SO 0410.

Maes y Gawnen: The reed stone. SN 9013.

Maesderwen: *Field of oak tree.* A house near the village of Llanfrynach. The house was built early in the 19th century. The remains of a Roman villa nearby were discovered in 1783 which may have been built in the third century during the reign of the 'Gallic' Emperors. A possible prehistoric tomb was found during the excavations, containing some human bones and fragments of an urn which may originate from the Bronze Age. In a field on the estate, called 'Cae Croff', according to legend, treasure is concealed and anyone attempting to dig it up would be frightened by 'apparitions' and some would be 'running mad' and others 'lamed.' SO 0625.

Mannog Cefn y Fan Foel: *High ridge of the bare peak.* SN 8121.

Mawnbwll Lloi: *Calves peat-bog pond.* SN 8125.

Mawnbwll: *Peat-bog pond.* SN 7924.

Mawnbwll-du Mawr: *Great black peat-bog pond.* SN 8027.

Mawnog Carnau Gwŷs: *Peat-bog cairns.* SN 8119.

Maen Llia

Meity Fechan: *Little mid-house.* SN 8425.

Moel Penderyn: *Bare bird's head hill.* Probably describes a topographical feature of the hill. SN 9308.

Moel Feity: *Mid-house bare hill.* SN 8422.

Moel Gornach: *Bare stack hill.* Moel Gornach is also known as Garreg Lwyd: *Grey stone.* SN 7418.

Myarth: P*lace in wooded slope.* SO 1720.

Myddfai: *Place in the hollow.* The village of Myddfai is famous for the Physicians of Myddfai Herbalists. The history probably originates in the 12th century with Rhiwallon, who was the personal physician to the Lord Rhys, and his three sons Cadwgan, Griffith and Einon were given land in the village of Myddfai and established a centre for herbal medicine and treatment. See also Llyn y Fan Fach for the legend of the Lady of the Lake and the Physicians of Myddfai. SN 7730.

Mynydd: *mountain*

Mynydd Bach Trecastell: Little, at Trecastell. Trecastell means *homestead by the castle.* The site of Bronze Age round barrows and a stone circle. It is also the location of the Roman Camps of Y Pigwn; *The Cone Peak*, on the Roman road from Brecon to Llanymddyfri. SN 8330.

Mynydd Brith: Brindled. SO 2740.

Mynydd Bychan: Little. Site of a round barrow which was a principal burial monument during the earlier Bronze Age. SO 1932.

Mynydd Du, Y: Black. SN 6816.

Mynydd Illtud: Illtud was a 6th century saint. Mynydd Illtud is found on common land to the north of the Beacons, where Illtud founded a church, Capel Illtud, now demolished. It is also the reputed burial place of Illtud where a vigil used to be held before the feast day of Illtud, 'Bedd Gwyl Illtud', on the 6th of November. The monastery at Llanilltud Fawr, where St. Illtud's Church now stands, was founded by Illtud. It was a monastic place of learning and some of his notable pupils included, St. David, Gildas, Teilo and King Maelgwn of Gwynedd. It is also understood Illtud may have founded the monastery at Caldey and that one of his former pupils, Samson, became its second abbott. SN 9625.

Mynydd Llangatwg: Llangatwg mountain. See Llangatwg. SO 1814.

Mynydd Llangors: *Llangors mountain.* Site of Neolithic and Bronze Age cairns. See Llangors. SO 1526.

Mynydd Llangynidr: *Llangynidr mountain. See Llangynidr.* SO 1214.

Mynydd Llanwenarth: *Llanwenarth mountain.* See Llanwenarth. SO 2616.

Mynydd Llysiau: Of herbs. SO 2027.

Mynydd Myddfai: *Myddfai mountain.* See Myddfai. SN 8029.

Mynydd Pen-cyrn: Of the summit tops or cairns. Site of cairns. SO 1914.

Mynydd Rheinallt: Rheinallt is a personal name. The area is the site of coal and iron ore workings dating from the 18th century. SO 2012.

Mynydd Troed: *Foot (shaped) mountain.* SO 1728.

Mynydd Wysg: *Wysg mountain/Usk mountain.* See afon Wysg. SN 8226.

Mynydd y Garn: Of the cairn mountain. Area of abandoned settlements, hut circles, stock enclosures and Bronze Age burial cairns. SN 9513.

Mynydd y Glog: Of the cliff. Site of Bronze Age cairn cemetery. SN 9708.

Mynydd y Llan: *The parish mountain.* SN 7924.

Nant: *stream/brook*

Nant Aber-nant: At the confluence of a stream. SO 0011.

Mynydd Illtud with Pen y Fan in the distance

Nant Alis: *Alis's stream* – Alis may be a personal name. SN 7427.

Nant Brân: Crow. See afon Brân. SO 2725.

Nant Brith: Speckled. SN 8429.

Nant Bwch: Buck. A tributary of the afon Honddu. SO 2332.

Nant Bwrefwr: SO 0518.

Nant Byfre: Babbling. The Swansea to Brecon railway route passed this way. SN 8616.

Nant Cadlan: Battlefield. SN 9609.

Nant Caeforys: At Morys's field. SN 7726.

Nant Callan: Hazel. Callan may derive from collen which means hazel. A tributary of the afon Taf Fechan. SO 0614.

Nant Car: It is thought 'car' may be derived from 'carrog' an old Welsh word for torrent. SO 0212.

Nant Cefn-y-maes: At the ridge of the field. SN 9911.

Nant Ceiliog: Cockerel. SN 8113.

Nant Celynnog: Holly-grove. SN 7024.

Nant Cil y Fforch: At the shelter of the fork. SN 9120.

Nant Cnewr fawr: *Great 'cnewr' stream.* SN 9022.

Nant Coch: Red. SN 8023.

Nant Cou: In a hollow. SN 9115.

Nant Craig Cwm-clyd: At the sheltered-valley rock. SN 7929

Nant Crinog: Parched. SN 8526.

Nant Crynfe: Withered. SN 7524.

Nant Cwm Clyd: In the sheltered valley. SN 7830.

Nant Cwm Du: In the dark valley. SN 9321.

Nant Cwm Gu: In the narrow valley. SO 1920.

Nant Cwm Llwch: In the lake valley. SO 0024.

Nant Cwm moel: In the bare valley. SO 0311.

Nant Cwmbyddar: In the deaf valley. SN 8614.

Nant Cwm-du: In the dark valley. SN 6823.

Nant Cwmothlwn: In the bare, scouring valley. SN 8024.

Nant Cwm-porth: At the valley entrance. SN 9517.

Nant Cwmtawel: In the quiet valley. SN 6819.

Nant Cynafon: Higher up than the river. SO 0718.

Nant Cynwyn: Head of white. SO 0322.

Nant Cyw: Chicken or foal. SN 7913.

Nant Ddu: Black/dark. The stream flows

Mynydd Troed

into the Taf Fawr below Cantref Reservoir. Nant Ddu is a hamlet which is part of the Llanfrynach Community Council. **Capel Nant Ddu:** *Nant Ddu chapel*. Rededicated as St. Mary's, demolished in 1998. It is recorded in the 1851 census as the chapel-of-ease to the Parish of Cantref consisting of the Cantref and Nant Ddu Chapelry with a population of 124 males and 113 females. SO 0014.

Nant Dwfn: Deep. SN 7119.

Nant Dwin: *Deep stream*. Dwin may derive from dwfn meaning *deep*. SN 7120.

Nant Fechan: Little. SN 8919.

Nant Ffynnon fawr: Of the great spring. SN 8514.

Nant Ffynnonelin: From Elin's well. SN 9912.

Nant Ffynnon-wen: White spring. SN 7621.

Nant Fydd: Fydd may derive from ffydd which means faith in Welsh. SN 7314.

Nant Ganol: Middle/central. SN 9516; SO 2233.

Nant Garlen Fawr: Garlen may derive from corlan which means a sheepfold or pen. The site of an enclosure is located in this area. SN 9418.

Nant Garw: Turbulent. SN 7216.

Nant y Gerdinen: By the mountain ash. SN 9720.

Nant Gihirych: Ridged. SN 8919.

Nant Goch: Red. SN 7825; SO 0016.

Nant Gwenllan: *Gwenllan's stream*. SN 7323.

Nant Gwinau: Brown. 7912; SN 7014 SO 0113.

Nant Gwrach: Witch. SN 7527.

Nant Gwyn: White. SN 7315.

Nant Gwythwch: Gwythwch is an old word in Welsh for wild pig. Site of a prehistoric hut circle. SN 6717.

Nant Henwen: Old white. SN 8329.

Nant Hepste-fechan: Little, dark. See afon Hepste. SN 9614.

Nant Hywel: *Hywel's stream*. SO 2533.

Nant Isaf: Lower. SN 8014; SO 2332.

Nant Llech Isaf: Lower rock or slab. SN 8613.

Nant Llech pellaf: Furthest rock or slab. SN 8713.

Nant Llechau: Rocks or slates. SN 8218.

Nant y Llestri: Vessels – may refer to the stone cairns found in this cairnfield. SO 0621.

Nant Lloi: Calves. SN 8125.

Nant Lluestau: Encampments. SN 8020.

Sgŵd Henryd on Nant Llech

Nant Llwch: Lake. SN 9615.

Nant Llwyn yr enwyn: The buttermilk grove. SO 1918.

Nant Llysiog: Llysiog may derive from llysieuog which can mean herbal. It is the site of a menhir or standing stone and a cairn. SO 0215.

Nant Llywarch: Llywarch is a personal name and may refer to a 6th century prince and poet. It is the site of hut circles, a Bronze or Iron Age settlement. SN 9616.

Nant Lwch: Lwch is probably a corruption of llwch which means lake. SN 9617.

Nant Mags Adda: *Mags Adam's stream.* SN 7421.

Nant Mawr: Great. SN 9515.

Nant Melyn: Yellow. Location of quarry worked in the 19th century for building stone. SN 7115;. SN 8123; SN 9807.

Nant Menascin: *Stream flowing to the Usk.* Theophilus Jones in his History of Breconshire, claims 'me' in Welsh, similar to 'meo' in Latin, means to flow, signifies a liquid. He maintains 'hascin' is a corruption of 'wyscin', a sreamlet, the diminutive of 'wy' or 'wysk', the latter probably derives from wysg, the Welsh word for usk. The source of Nant Menascin is from Cwm Oergwm below Fan y Big and it joins the Usk near Pencelli: *Grovesend.* SO 0624.

Nant Moel: Bare. SN 9707.

Nant Morlais: Loud. SO 0711.

Nant Mydan: *Mydan's stream.* SN 7832.

Nant Ochram: At the side (canal). SO 2809.

Nant Oesglyn: At the old glen. SN 7120.

Nant Pant glas: Green hollow. SN 7321.

Nant Pedol: Horseshoe. SN 6914.

Nant Pedwar: *Four stream.* SN 8427.

Nant Pennig: Pennig may derive from penaig an old obscure word in Welsh for chief. The site of a long hut prehistoric settlement. The stream flows into the Beacons Reservoir. SN 9719.

Nant Plas-y-gors: The marsh grange. SN 9215.

Nant Pyrgad: *Pyrgad's stream.* SO 1015.

Nant Rhuddel: Rubric or crimson. SN 7230.

Nant Rhyd-ddu: Dark ford. SO 0313.

Nant Sali Morys: According to local tradition Sali Morys lived in the parish of Llanddeusant. Sali used to carry farm produce in baskets over the mountain to Ystrdgynlais and Brynaman. Following a heavy storm on the mountain, her body

Nant Menascin

was found near the stream which was named after her. SN 7820.

Nant Sere: *Sere stream.* SO 0223.

Nant Sych: Dry. SO 0108.

Nant Sychbant: Dried up hollow. SO 0110.

Nant Tarthwynni: White mist. SO 0919.

Nant Tarw: Bull. Site of stone circle and cairns. SN 8225.

Nant Tawe Fechan: *Little Tawe stream.* Site of a burnt mound, a Bronze Age settlement. SN 8318.

Nant Tŷ-bach: At the little house. SN 8025.

Nant Tywynni: Shining. SN 8517.

Nant Uchaf: Upper. SO 2233.

Nant War-rhaca: At the back of the narrow hill. SN 7727.

Nant Wern ddu: At the dark meadow. The stream joins the Taf Fawr. SO 0115.

Nant y Beudy: At the cowshed. SN 7930.

Nant y Bryn-bach: By the little hill. SN 9017.

Nant y Bwllfa: At the pool/well. SN 9507.

Nant y Cadno: The fox. SN 8222.

Nant y Cared: The Cared stream. SN 9212.

Nant y Clochydd: The sexton. SN 9921.

Nant y coetgae: The woodfield. A field cleared of forest. Coedgae or coed cae has a meaning which is particular to south Wales and describes a wooded area on the steep upper slopes of the valleys. SN 8419.

Nant y Coy: *The Coy stream.* SO 2325.

Nant y Creigiau: At the crags. SN 8024.

Nant y Cwm: In the valley. SN 9016.

Nant y Cwrier: The currier. Site of small cairn. SN 9716.

Nant y Ddraenen: The thorns. SN 7819; SN 9518; SO 1417.

Nant y Deri: The oak-trees. SN 9607.

Nant y Ffeldydd: 'Ffeld' may derive from ffald which means sheepfold in Welsh. 'ydd' may derive from esydd an old obscure Welsh word for dwelling or home. SN 9416.

Nant y Ffrwd: Ffrwd can describe a torrent or a lesser brook. SO 0511.

Nant y Foel: By the bare hill. SN 7925.

Nant y Gaseg: The mare. SN 9420.

Nant y Glais: Clais which mutates to glais in Welsh means stream bed. SO 0410.

Nant y Gloesydd: At the coal dwelling. SO 0418.

Nant y Grawen: The rough meadow. SO 0111.

Nant y Gwair: The hay. SN 9520.

Nant y Gwared: Gwared may derive from gwaered meaning to descend. SN 8315.

Sgŵd Isaf Clun-gwyn on Mellte river

Nant y Gwartheg: The cattle. SO 2424.

Nant y Llechau: At the stone slabs. SN 9010.

Nant y Llyn: The lake. SN 7717; SN 8420.

Nant y moch: The pigs. SN 8916.

Nant y Wenynen: The bee. SO 1118.

Nant y Wern: The marsh. SO 0311.

Nant yr Offeiriad: The priest. SN 9920.

Nant yr Annell: Annell may derive from Ariannell which is a personal name or the word for silver. Water from afon Annell was diverted via aqueduct to the Roman gold mine at Dolaucothi which means; *Meadows beside the river Cothi.* SO 2434.

Nant yr Eiddil: The slender. SO 1531.

Nant yr Eira: The snowy. Site of a prehistoric copper mine and a 19th century lead mine. SN 9817.

Nant yr Erydr: The ploughs. SN 8322.

Nant yr Esgyrn: The bones. SN 9416.

Nant yr Helyg: The willows. So 2329.

Nant yr Hen Heol: By the old road. SO 0319.

Nant yr Hiddl: The copious. SN 7627.

Nant yr Ŵydd: The goose. SN 8618; SN 9316.

Nant yr Wysg: Fish-filled. The Usk stream in English. SN 8420.

Nant yr Ychen: The oxen. Site of a prehistoric round cairn. SN 9617; SO 0715.

Nant yr Ysgwydd: The shoulder. SN 7822.

Nant Ysgallen: The thistle. SO 2137.

Nant Ystwyth: Meandering. SN 9320.

Nantllannerch: The clearing/glade. SO 0821.

Nantywenynen: The bees. SN 9314.

Nedd Fechan: *Little shining stream.* Nedd is derived from the ancient Brythoneg 'nida' meaning shining stream. SN 9110.

Nentydd Blaen Twrch: *Streams at the source of the river Twrch.* See afon Twrch. SN 8121.

Nentydd Gorlan Lwyd: *Streams at the grey fold.* SN 8020.

Neuadd Buckland: *Buckland Hall.* Buckland Hall was the home of Henry Seymour Berry, Lord Buckland, 1877 – 1928. He was a generous benefactor to the people of Merthyr Tydfil and his statue stands outside the central library. SO 1321.

Odyn-fach: *Little kiln.* SO 0812.

Ogof Fawr: *Great cave.* SN 9809.

Ogof Fawr: *Great cave – Chartist cave.* The name Chartist cave is derived from the Chartists using the cave to store weapons

Nant y Ffin tavern named after local stream

before their march on Newport in 1839. SO 1215.

Ogof yr Esgyrn: *The bones cave.* Cave in Dan yr Ogof. SN 8316.

Oldcastle: *Hengastell.* SO 3224.

Ollwyn: *Ash grove.* Name of the mountain. SN 9908.

Pâl y Cwrt: *The courtyard digger.* Site of silica sand quarries closed in the 1950s. SN 6718.

Pant: *hollow/glen/dingle*
Pant y Wern: The alder marsh. SN 9914.
Pant Brwynog: Rushy. SN 9817.
Pant Draenog: Hedgehog. SO 2113.
Pant Ffald-fach: Little sheepfold. SN 9416.
Pant Gilfach-wen: White creek. SN 9518.
Pant Llwyd: Grey or holy. SO 1317.
Pant Mawr: Great. SN 8914; SO 2013.
Pant Meddygon: *Dingle of the physicians.* Site of cairn. The area is associated with the legend of Llyn y Fan fach. SN 8028.
Pant Nant fforchog: Forked stream. SN 6918.
Pant Serthfa: At the steep place. SO 1116.
Pant Sychbant: Dry valley. Site of cairns. SN 9809.
Pant Tyle Gwyn: White hill. SN 7922.

Pant y Bwlch: Under the pass. SN 8121.
Pant y Creigiau: The rocks. SO 0616.
Pant y Ddwyros: Of the two moors. Site of a cairn. SN 8129.
Pant y Drenewydd: The Newtown. SN 7219.
Pant y Gadair: Of the mound. Site of prehistoric hut circle. SN 9912.
Pant y Gelynnen: The holly. SO 0721.
Pant y rhiw: The steep slope. Location of an adventure centre. SO 1018.
Pant y Waun: The marshy ground. SN 9816.
Pant yr Esgair: Long ridge. SN 7719.
Pantyffynnon: Of the spring. SN 7319.

Patrisio: *Saint Isio's or Issui's shrine/resting place.* A holy well at the bottom of a hill near the medieval church is the reputed cell of St. Issui, an early Christian hermit and preacher who was murdered at the place. The original name of the place was Merthyr Issui; *Issui the martyr.* (Patrishow) SO 2722.

Pen: *top/head/summit/end*
Pen Allt Mawr: Of the great slope. SO 2024.

Pannau farm near Llanfynach

Pen Allt: Of the slope. SN 7525.

Pen Bryn Mawr: Of the great hill. SN 6816.

Pen Bwlch Glasgwm: Of the green valley pass. SO 0916.

Pen Caenewydd: Of the new field. 7828.

Pen Cerrig calch: Of the limestone. Site of Bronze Age cairns. SO 2122.

Pengenffordd: *end of the ridgeway.* SO 1730.

Pen Gloch-y-pibwr: Of the piper's bell. SO 2023.

Pen Gwyllt Meirch: Of the wild ridge of horses. SO 2424.

Pen Milan: Of the fierce hill. Milan may derive from the Welsh word milain which means fierce, grim, vicious. SN 9923.

Pen Moelallt: Of the bare hill. A community woodland. SO 0009.

Pen Rhiw ddu: Of the black slope. Site of a cairn. SN 7219.

Pen Rhiw goch: Of the red hill. SN 7821.

Pen Rhiw Ifor: Of Ifor's hill. SO 2511.

Pen Rhiw-calch: Of the limestone hill. SO 1017.

Pen Rhos Dirion: Of the gentle moor. Trig point. SO 2033.

Pen Tir: Headland. SO 1725.

Pen Twyn Glas: Of the green hill. SO 2125.

Pen Twyn Mawr: Of the great hill. Site of a cairn. SO 2426.

Pen Tyle: Of the hill. SN 7824.

Pen y Bicws: Of the peak. Pen y Bicws is the site of three cairns and it is also known as Trichrug which means *three cairns*. SN 6922.

Pen y Bylchau: Of the passes. SN 8130.

Pen y cae: Of the field. The village was named from a house, Pen y cae, in the 19th century. SN 8413.

Pen y crug: Of the cairn. The site of a large iron age hillfort. SO 0230.

Pen y Fâl: Of the mill. Mynydd Pen y Fâl has also been described as a mountain at the top of the peak. (Sugar Loaf) SO 2718.

Pen y Fan: Of the ridge. Formerly known as Cadair Arthur: *Arthur's chair.* The highest peak in southern Wales at 886 metres. It is also the site of a Bronze Age cairn on the summit. SO 0121.

Pen y Gadair Fawr: Of the great chair. The second highest peak in the Black Mountains. SO 2228.

Pen y Gaer: Of the fort. SO 0615.

Pen y gaer: Of the fort. A Roman fort was built here in about AD 70 and remained in use until around AD 130. SO 1621.

Pen y Manllwyn: Of the fine grove. SO 2031.

Pen Milan and Cwm Llwch

Pen y Porth: Of the gateway. SN 9312.
Pen yr Helyg: Of the willow. SN 7616.
Pencelli: Of the grove. Celli can also mean copse or woodland. The ruins of Pencelli Castle still stand in the village. It was built by Ralph Baskerville in the late 11th century. The castle was seized by Reginald Broase in 1215 and later captured by rebelling Welsh forces in 1233. Roger Mortimer jnr. acquired the castle in 1273. However, it fell into decay following its capture by King Edward 11 in 1322. SO 0925.
Penderyn: Of the bird's head. SN 9408.
Pendre: Of the settlement. SO 0429.
Pengenffordd: Of the ridgeway - probably 'g(c)efnffordd'. SO 1730.
Pennorth: Of a hillside. Pennorth may derive from the corrupt spelling of pennarth. SO 1125.
Penpont: *Bridge end*. The location of a Grade 1 listed house built in the 17th century. SN 9728.
Pentir Blaencennen: *Headland at the source of the river Cennen.* Cennen may be a personal name or lichen stoned river. SN 6918.

Pentre'r Felin: *The mill village.* SN 9230.

Pentregronw: *Gronw's homestead.* SN 7928.
Pentwyn garthen: *Head of the dune hill.* SN 7731.
Penwern: Of the alder. SO 0028.
Penwyllt: Of the wild land. SN 8515.

Picws Du: *Black peak.* A Bronze Age round barrow is found on the summit. SN 8121.
Plas-y-gors: *the place at the marsh.* The site of a Roman marching camp. SN 9216.
Pont yr Efail: *The smithy's bridge.* SO 2313.
Ponsticill: *Stile bridge.* SO 0511.

Pont: *bridge*
Pont Aber-car: On the Car stream – fast flowing stream. SO 0012.
Pont ar Daf: On the Taf. SN 9819.
Pont ar Hydfer: On the Hydfer river – brave-flowing river. SN 8627.
Pont ar Lia: On the river Llia – lapping river. SN 9314.
Pontarllechau: On the river Llechach (stone filled river). SN 7224.
Pont ar Wysg: On the river Wysg (Usk) – fish-filled river. SN 8127.
Pont Blaen-y-glyn: At the head of the valley. Site of waterfalls. SO 0617.

Pontsticil reservoir

Pont Cadwgan: *Cadwgan's bridge.* SO 2625.

Pont Clydach: On the river Clydach – river that flows over a flat, rocky bed. SN 7319.

Pont Cwm y fedwen: At the birch valley. SO 0416.

Pont Cwm: *Valley bridge.* SN 9014.

Pont Cwrt yr argoed: At the woodland court. SO 1937.

Pont Garreg: S*tone bridge.* SO 0215.

Pont Gihirych: *Bridge at the peak.* SN 8821.

Pont Gwilym: *Gwilym's bridge.* SO 0403.

Pont Llysiog: On the Llysiog stream. See Nant Llysiog. SO 0014.

Pont Melin Fach: By the little mill. Bridge on the Nedd Fechan River. SN 9010.

Pont Nant Ddu: On the black/dark stream. See Nant Ddu. SO 0014.

Pont Nant Gwinau: On the brown stream. 0012.

Pont Nant y moch: On the pig's stream. SN 8619.

Pont Newydd: *New bridge.* SN 8828.

Pont Parc Owen: At Owen's field. SN 6819.

Pont Rhyd y cnau: At the hazel tree ford. SN 9111.

Pontsticill: *Stile bridge.* SO 0511.

Pont Tal y Maes: At the end of the field. The bridge spans the Grwyne Fach. SO 2226.

Pont Tywynni: On the nant Tywynni – shining stream. SN 8517.

Pont Wingon: *'Wingon' bridge.* SN 8727.

Pont y Blaenau: In the uplands. SO 1826.

Pont y Felin: By the mill. SN 9314.

Pont y Llwyn: By the grove. SO 0416.

Pont yr Offeiriad: *The Clergyman's bridge.* SN 8414.

Pontsenni: On the river Senni. The remains of a castle built by Llywelyn ap Gruffudd in the 13th century stands to the west of Sennybridge. Another castle built by Llywelyn ap Gruffudd stood at Cwm Camlais and it also possibly became the castle of Einion Sais of Penpont. (Sennybridge). SN 9228.

Porth yr ogof: *Portal/entrance to the cave.* SN 9212.

Pwll: *pool*

Pwll Calch: Lime. SN 7628.

Pwll Coch: Red. SO 1615.

Pwll Crochan: Cauldron. SN 9207.

Pwll Cynrig: Cynrig. See Abercynrig. SN 7820.

Pwll Derw: Oaken. SN 9412.

Pwll Du: Black. SN 9112; SO 2411.

Pwll Dudrwyth: Black infused. SN 7118.

Pwll Dwfn: Deep. Pothole cave. SN 8316.

Pwll Figyn Fawr: Great marsh. SO1913.

Pwll Gwy-rhoc: The meandering river 'rhoc'. SO 1815.

Pwll Morlais: Morlais suggests a loud stream. SO 0711.

Pwll Pant mawr: Great hollow. SN 8814.

Pwll Pen-ffordd-goch: At the bottom of the red road. It is also known locally as 'Keeper's pond'. SO 2510.

Pwll Swnd: Sand. A cave. SN 7618.

Pwll Taf: *Taf pool.* SO 0208.

Pwll y Cawr: *The giant's pond.* SN 8315.

Pwll y Cig: Meat. A Bronze Age cairn. SN 8118.

Pwll y Felin: By the mill. SN 9412.

Pwll y Wrach: *The witch's pool.* Brecknock Wildlife Trust Nature Reserve. An ancient woodland and waterfall. SO 1632.

Pwll yr henllyn: *The old lake pond.* SN 8021.

Pwll yr Wydden Fach: *Little pond at the wood.* SN 8215.

Pwll yr Wydden: *Pond at the wood.* Site of a round cairn. SN 8215.

Pwllymerched: *The girls pond.* SN 7414.

Pwll-y-rhyd: At the ford. A cave. SN 9014.

Pyllau'r Fai: *The field ponds.* SN 6716.

Rhiangoll: *Lost part stream.* SO 1930.

Rhiw: *slope*

Rhiw Fer: Short. SN 7822.

Rhiw Wen: White. SN 7319; SO 2135.

Rhiw yr Ysgyfarnog: Of the hare. SO 0119.

Rhiwiau: *Slopes.* SN 7526.

Rhiwlas: Green. SN 7822.

Rhongyr Isaf: *Lower drove end.* SN 8514.

Rhos: *moor*

Rhos Dringarth: Battlefield hill. SN 9520.

Rhos Fawr: Great. SO 1934.

Rhos Llechach: Stony. SN 8025.

Rhosaman: Piglet. SN 7314.

Rhuddnant: *Brown stream.* SN 8723.

Rhyd: *ford*

Rhyd ap Sion: *Ap Sion's ford.* The identity of ap Sion is not known, although 'ap' in Welsh means son of Sion. SN 9715.

Rhyd Uchaf: Highest. Site of a cairn. SN 9218; SN 9817.

Rhyd y Saint: Of the saints. SN 7125.

Sgŵd Ddwli

Rhyd-wen Fach: Little white. SN 8223.
Rhyd-wen Fawr: Great white. SN 8323.

Saith Maen: *Seven stones.* Row of seven Bronze Age stones near Craig y Nos Castle, aligned in the direction of the Cerrig Duon stone circle. Cerrig duon means *black stones*. SN 8315.

Sarn Helen: *Causeway or Roman road named after Helen.* Elen or Helen was princess of Segontium, a Roman stronghold in Caernarfon and the wife of Macsen Wledig – Magnus Maximus, the Roman governor of Britain in the 4th century. SN 9625.

Sawdde Fechan: *The lesser Sawdde.* A tributary of afon Sawdde – see afon Sawdde. SN 7522.

Sgethrog: *Scattered or craggy settlement.* The word sgethrog is derived from sgathrog which means rough, craggy, rocky. Sgethrog was a manorial centre in the Middle Ages. (Scethrog). SO 1025.

Sgŵd: *waterfall/cascade*
Sgŵd Clun-gwyn: At the white meadow. The upper of the three waterfalls on the afon Mellte. SN 9210.

Sgŵd Ddu: *Dark or black fall.* (Waterfall on the Afon Haffes) SN 8217.
Sgŵd Ddwli: *Gushing fall.* (Waterfall on the Nedd Fechan) SN 9009.
Sgŵd Einion Gam: Einion is a personal name and cam can mean crooked or bent. SO 8909.
Sgŵd Gwladys: Gwladys is a personal name and the falls may be named after Gwladys the daughter of Brychan Brycheiniog, the ancient ruler of Brycheiniog/Breconshire. SO 8909.
Sgŵd Henryd: At the old ford. (Waterfall on the Nant Llech) SN 8512.
Sgŵd Isaf Clun-gwyn: *Lower fall of the white meadow.* Middle of the three falls on the afon Mellte. SN 9210.
Sgŵd y Pannwr: *Fall of the fuller or fall of the woollen washer.* Lowermost of the three falls on the afon Mellte. SN 9210.
Sgŵd yr Eira: Snowy. (Waterfall on the Afon Hepste) SN 9209.

Sinc y Gïedd: *The Gïedd sink.* See afon Gïedd. SN 8117.
Slwch: *The name slwch is derived from 'sloh' an old English word meaning 'muddy place'.* It is the site of an Iron Age fort which was formerly known as Pen cefn y gaer: *Ridge at the head of the fort.* SO 0528.

Sgŵd yr Eira

Storey Arms: The name Storey originates from the name of the owner of the property, Anthony Mervin Storey, in the 19th century. He was a JP and the deputy lieutenant of Breconshire. The original Storey Arms Inn was demolished in 1924 and it is now an outdoor education centre, owned by Cardiff Council. SN 9820.

Table Mountain: The summit of this mountain is the site of an Iron Age fort and was originally known as Crug Hywel: *Hywel's hill* – from which the town takes its name. The Hywel in question may not be Hywel Dda, a king of the 10th century and may refer to Hywel ap Rhys, king of Morgannwg 856 – 886. SO 2220.

Taf Fechan: *Litttle river Taf.* The river Taf rises south of Pen y Fan and runs through the Neuadd reservoirs. The Taf Fawr and the Taf Fechan rivers join near Godre'r Coed (*Bottom of the wood*) at Cefn Coed y Cymer, north of Merthyr Tydfil and they then form the River Taf which flows out to sea at Cardiff. The Taf Fechan Reservoir was completed in 1927. The 15th century Dolygaer Church (Capel Taf Fechan) and Bethlehem Congregational Chapel together with some cottages were submerged by the reservoir. SO 0220.

Tair Bull: *Dwellings of the Bwl or Bull Inn.* Houses in the village of Libanus. (Tai'r Bull). SN 9926.

Tair Carn Isaf: *Lower three cairns.* Site of Bronze Age burial cairns. SN 6816.

Tair Carn Uchaf: *Higher three cairns.* SN 6917.

Tal: *head/end/brow*

Tal y Llyn: Of the lake. SO 1027.

Talcen y Garn: Of the cairn. Site of cairn. SN 9515.

Talgarth: Of the ridge. Castell Dinas or Bwlch y Ddinas, a Norman castle built in the second half of the 11th century was located 3 miles to the south-east of Talgarth. The castle was once the site of a hill-fort and it was the highest site of a castle in England and Wales at the head of the Rhiangoll, Grwyne and Honddu valleys. It was seized by Llywelyn ap Gruffudd in 1262/63 and later passed to the English Crown in 1322 and fell into ruin. Tŵr Talgarth: *Talgarth Tower*, the remains of a 12th century castle which stands over the brook in the middle of the village. Howel Harris (1714 – 1773), a leader of the Welsh Methodist revival is buried at Talgarth. SO 1533.

Taf Fechan

Talsarn: Of the causeway. SN 7726; SO 2431.

Talybont ar Wysg: Of the bridge on the river Wysg (Usk). SO 1122.

Talylan: Of the church. SN 7024.

Tarren yr Esgob: *The bishop's ridge.* SO 2331.

Tarren Tormwnt: *Belly-hill ridge.* SO 0415.

The Arwallt: *On the hill-side.* SO 3318.

Tir-yr-onnen: *The ash tree land.* SN 9612.

Tomen Llechach: *Rock mound.* SN 7925.

Ton-teg: *Fair meadow.* SN 9615.

Tor glas: *Green/grassy hill.* SO 0319.

Tor: *hill*

Tor y Bigwns: Cone shaped. SO 0120.

Tor y Foel: Bare. SN 9408; SO 1119.

Tormwnt: Mount. SO 0314.

Torpantau: At the hollows. The Torpantau railway station was the highest station on the Merthyr Tydfil to Brecon railway line which closed in 1963. The Torpantau or Beacons tunnel is located north of the station. SO 0418.

Trallwng, Y: *Marshy place.* (Trallong). SN 9629.

Begwns

Trawsnant uchaf: *Upper strong-flowing stream.* SN 8318.

Trawsnant: *Strong-flowing stream.* SN 7922; SN 8317; SO 0414.

Tre: *town/settlement*

Tre'r Esgob: Of the bishop. SN 8729.

Treberfydd: Treberfydd may derive from treberfedd which means middle or centre dwelling/residence or town. Treberfydd is a Grade 1 Listed 19th century gothic 'Tudor Revival House.' SO 1225.

Trecastell: By the castle. The castle was probably built by the Norman lord of Brycheiniog, Bernard de Neufemarche in the 11th century. It was besieged by Welsh insurgents during the 12th century. The site of the castle is located above the river Usk on the route between Aberhonddu/Brecon and Llanymddyfri. (Trecastle). SN 8829

Trefecca: Beca's – from the biblical name Rebecca. The birthplace of Howel Harris (1714 – 1773) the Methodist leader, where he began his preaching in around 1735. It is also the site of Coleg Trefeca, the training centre and retreat for the Presbyterian Church in Wales. SO 1432.

Tretŵr: With the tower. The castle at Tretŵr was probably built at the turn of the 12th and 13th century and was occupied by the first Baron Picard. His son Roger was a supporter of Llewelyn ap Gruffudd, and in spite of this act of treason against King Henry 111, the family survived until its demise in the early part of the 13th century. Tretŵr was then occupied by the Bluets of Raglan as their manor house and gradually deteriorated. SO 1821.

Trichrug: *Three summits.* Site of a cairn. SN 6923.

Tro: *turn (in the road/path)*
Tro Rhiwgrugos: At the heather hill. SN 7119.
Tro Tir y Gât: At the gate land. SN 7319.
Tro'r Derlwyn: At the oak grove. SN 7215.
Tro'r Fan Foel: At the bare peak. SN 8222.

Troedrhiwfelin: *Mill at the foot of the hill.* SN 7834.
Troed-y-rhiw: *Foot of the hill.* SO 1017.
Twmpa: *Tump.* Otherwise known as Lord Hereford's Knob. So 2235.
Tŵr Cennen: *Tower at river Cennen.* See afon Cennen. SN 6721.
Tŵr Pen-cyrn: *Tower at head of cairn.* SO 2014.

Twyn: *peak/hill*
Twyn Mwyalchod: Of the blackbirds. SO 0216.
Twyn Brynffaldau: Of the sheepfolds. SN 8613.
Twyn ceiliog: Of the cock. SN 8827; SO 0912.
Twyn Cerrig Cenau: Cenau can mean a small animal and may refer to shape of this rocky outcrop. SN 8923.
Twyn Cil-rhew: Of the ice recess. SO 0124.
Twyn Croes Gwallter: *Of Gwallter's cross.* SN 9414.
Twyn Croes: Of the cross. SO413.
Twyn Disgwylfa: Of the look-out. SN 8516; SO 1617.
Twyn Draintewion: Of the thick thorns. SN 7822.
Twyn Du: Black. SN 8316; SO 0820.
Twyn Dylluan ddu: Of the black owl. SN 9623.
Twyn Garreg-wen: Of the white rock. Site of Stone Age/Bronze Age round cairn. SN 9816.
Twyn Gwyn: White. SO 2718.
Twyn Henwen: The old white. SN 8330.
Twyn Llannan: By the little church. SN 7524.
Twyn Llangwilym: By Gwilym's church. SO 2215.

Twyn Llech: Rock. SO 2435.

Twyn Mawn: Peat. SN 7923.

Twyn Perfedd: Middle. SN 8325.

Twyn Pica: Pointed. The name of the waterfall. SO 0416.

Twyn Pwll Morlais: At the great stream pool. SO 0811.

Twyn Rhyblid: Rhyblid hill. SN 7828.

Twyn Spratt: Spratt hill. Site of disused limekiln. SN 8316.

Twyn Swnd: Sand. SN 7820.

Twyn Tal y Ddraenen: At top of the bramble. SN 8119.

Twyn Talycefn: At the top of the ridge. Site of cairn. SO 2232.

Twyn Walter: *Walter's hill.* SN 8317.

Twyn Wenallt: Of the wooded slope. SO 2413.

Twyn y Beddau: Of the graves. Site of Bronze Age round barrow cairn. SO 2438.

Twyn y Dyfnant: Of the ravine. SO 0123.

Twyn y Fan: By the peak. SN 7931.

Twyn y Ffald: The sheepfold. Disused limekiln built in 1825 and 1827. SN 8516.

Twyn y Gaer: Of the hill fort. Site of Iron Age hillfort. SN 9828.

Twyn y Garn: Of the cairn. SN 8825.

Twyn y Llyn: At the lake. SO 1015.

Twyn y Moch: Of the pig. SN 7414.

Twyn y Neuadd: Of the hall. SO 0219.

Twyn yr allt: Of the slope. SO 2916.

Twyn yr Esgair: Of the ridge. SN 8123.

Twyn yr Odynau: Of the limekilns. Site of round cairn and disused limekilns. SN 9515.

Twynau Gwynion: White. SO 0812.

Tyle: *hill/slope*

Tyle Brith: Speckled. SN 9919.

Tyle Du: Black. SN 7722.

Tyle Ffardding wood: Of the farthing wood. SO 2825.

Tyle Garw: Rough. SN 7717.

Tyle Gwyn: White. SN 7921.

Tyr Doppa: *Tower top.* SN 6720.

Upper Neuadd: The reservoir at Upper Neuadd was built during the Zulu War in 1902 and became known as the 'Zulu Reservoir'. It is also the site of a small ring cairn. SO 0219.

Vale of Grwyne: See afon Grwyne. SO 2523.

Waun: *moor/marshland/high meadow*

Waun Carn-y-defaid: Of the sheeps cairn. SO 2709.

Waun Ddu: Dark/black. SN 8230; SO 1816.

Waun Dywarch: Of the turf. SN 9515.
Waun fach: Little. SO 2130; SO1826.
Waun Fforest: Above/by the forest. SN 8124.
Waun Ffos-ddu: Of the black ditch. SN 7926.
Waun Fignen: Of the boggy marsh. SN 8218.
Waun Goch: Red. SO 2431.
Waun Haffes: *Haffes moor.* See afon Haffes. SN 8219.
Waun Lefrith: Milk. SN 7921.
Waun Leuci: Leuci is probably a corruption of Lleucu – a personal name. It is the site of a menhir or standing stone. SN 8621.
Waun Llywarch: Llywarch's moor. SN 9616.
Waun Lwyd fach: Little grey. SN 7018.
Waun Lwyd: Grey. SN 7319; SN 8124.
Waun Lysiog: L(l)ysiog may derive from llysieuog which can mean herbal. See nant Lysiog. SO 0216.
Waun Rydd: Free/Common. SO 0620; SO 0714.
Waun Sychlwch: Dry lake. SN 8022.
Waun Tincer: Of the tinker. Site of round cairn. SN 9614.
Waun Watcyn: *Watkin moor.* SO 2114.

Waun Wen: White. SO 0214; SO 2211.
Waun y Ddraenen: Of the thorn. SN 7515.
Waun y Gorlan: Of the sheepfold. SO 0618.
Waun y Groes: Of the cross. SN 8032.
Waun y Gwair: Of the hay. Site of round cairn. SO 0811.
Waun y Llyn: Of the lake. SN 8022.

Wenallt Fawr: The great white hillside. SN 7723.
Wern y Frân: *The crow's alder moor.* SO 0524.

Y Mynydd Du: *The Black Mountains.* SO 2331.
Y Dderi Fawr: *The great oak-trees.* SN 7425.
Y Fan: *The summit.* SO 2430.
Y Fforch: *The fork.* SO 0114.
Y Gaer Fach: *The lesser fortress.* SN 6824.
Y Gaer Fawr: *The greater fortress.* SN 6924.
Y Gaer: *The Fort.* The great Roman fort built by General Julius Frontinus in about AD 75. SN 9226; SN 9928; SO 0029.
Y Garn: *The Cairn.* SN 7025.
Y Gors: *The bog.* SN 8729.
Y Grib: *The ridge.* SO 1931/30.
Y Grug: *The mound.* SN 7834.

Y Mynydd Du

Y Gyrn: *The mountain peaks.* SN 9821.

Y Pigwn: *The cone peak.* Site of Roman marching camp. SN 8231.

Y Wern: *The marshland where alders grow.* SN 8613.

Ynys Crug: *Meadow hillock.* SN 6819.

Ynys Isaf: *Lower meadow.* SN 7911.

Ynyswen: *Fair meadow.* SN 8313.

Yr Allt: *The wooded hillside.* SN 9019; SN 9129.

Yr Allt: *The wooded hillside.* SO 0515.

Ysgyryd Fawr: *Greater (pile of) shards.* (The Skirrid). SO 3317.

Ystradfellte: *Vale of the river Mellte – lightning or fast river.* See afon Mellte. SN 9313.

Y Gyrn and Pen Milan (left) and Ysgyryd Fawr

References

A Guide to Ancient and Historic Wales, Clwyd and Powys: Helen Burnham.

A Study of Breconshire Place Names: Richard Morgan & R.F. Peter Powell.

Atlas Brycheiniog: Pwyllgor Addysg Brycheiniog 1958/59.

Bannau Brycheiniog A History of Place names: Malcolm Llywelyn.

Brycheiniog A History of Place Names: Malcolm Llywelyn.

Brycheiniog Vol. 11: Some Breconshire Place Names: Stephen J. Williams.

Brycheiniog Vol. 19: Notes on a Place-name. Element Peculiar to Breconshire: R.F. Peter Powell.

Brycheiniog Vol. 23: The Place Names of Devynock Hundred 111; Cantref & Glyn.

Castles of Breconshire: Paul Remfry.

Ein Cynefin/Where We Belong, Vol. 1 & 11: Editor Susan Brook.

Enwau Tir a Gwlad: Melville Richards.

Enwau'r Wlad: D. Geraint Lewis.

History of Breconshire: Theophilus Jones.

The Historic Taf Valleys: John Perkins, Jane Evans and Mary Gillham.

Prehistoric Sites of Breconshire: George Children and George Nash.

The Welsh Language and the 1891 Census: Gwenfair Parry & Mari A. Williams.

Vaynor A Study of the Welsh Countryside: Elwyn Bowen.

The Welsh Academy Encyclopaedia of Wales: Co-editors; John Davies, Nigel Jenkins, Menna Baines, Peredur I. Lynch. Published by University of Wales Press Cardiff 2008.

The Welsh Language and the 1891 Census: Gwenfair Parry & Mari A. Williams.

Welsh Place Names: Dewi Davies.

William Rees: The Brecknock Society.

Y Llyfr Enwau: D. Geraint Lewis.

Sgŵd Uchaf Clun-gwyn

Learning Welsh

1. Cwrs Mynediad
Entry course for beginners widely used in Welsh classes.

2. Cwrs Mynediad 4 cassettes. Cassettes to accompany the course book.

3. Welsh Learners Dictionary by Heini Gruffudd, published by Lolfa. A dictionary for Welsh learners with a grammar and guide on mutations.

4. A Dictionary of Welsh and English Idiomatic Phrases. Compiled by Alun Rhys Cownie. Published by University of Wales Press. An introduction to idiomatic Welsh for learners with a section on Welsh – English and English – Welsh.

5. Cerddi'r Cewri. Editor Islwyn Edwards, published by Gwasg Gomer. An introduction to some of the best twentieth century poetry in Welsh for the Welsh learner with a vocabulary and notes.

6. Ffrindiaith. Network of Welsh learners and speakers to facilitate practicing the language as individuals or in groups. A free online service. Contact: Ffrindiaith.org.

7. Lingo Newydd, published by Golwg. A quarterly magazine for Welsh learners. Available from lingonewydd@golwg.com or tel. 01570 423529.

8. Saysomethinginwelsh. A free online course accessed by contacting: saysomethinginwelsh.com.

Dragon carving in Patrisio church

BEST WALKS
IN THE
BEACON MOUNTAINS

* From short family walks
  to the highest peaks

* Lake, river and
  woodland walks also

www.carreg-gwalch.cymru

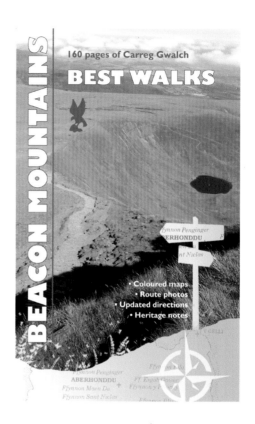

Best Walks
in
Glamorgan and Gwent

* Walks with heritage

* Panoramic views

* For all the family

www.carreg-gwalch.cymru

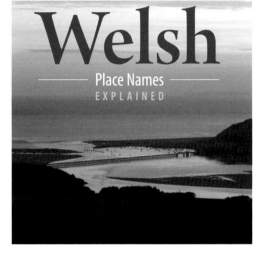

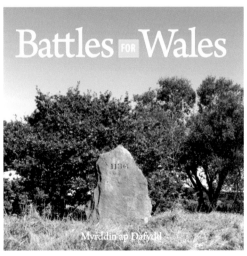

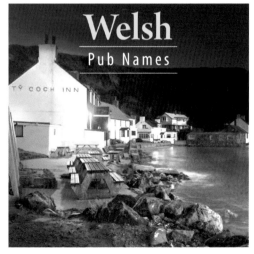

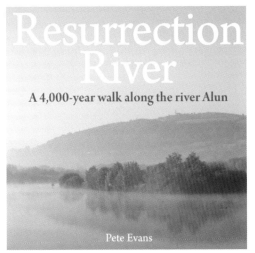

Resurrection River
A 4,000-year walk along the river Alun

Pete Evans

Snowdon
Villages and its
EXPLORED

Welsh Poetry
in translation

Howard Huws

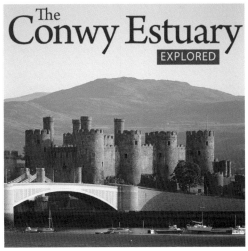

The Conwy Estuary
EXPLORED

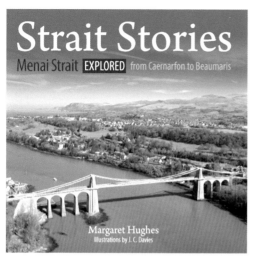

Strait Stories
Menai Strait EXPLORED from Caernarfon to Beaumaris

Margaret Hughes
Illustrations by J. C. Davies

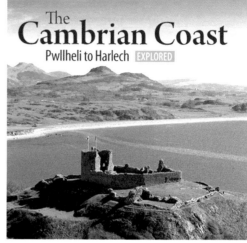

The Cambrian Coast
Pwllheli to Harlech EXPLORED

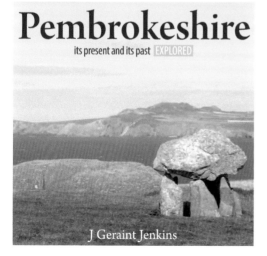

Pembrokeshire
its present and its past EXPLORED

J Geraint Jenkins

The Cambrian Coast
Harlech to Aberystwyth EXPLORED

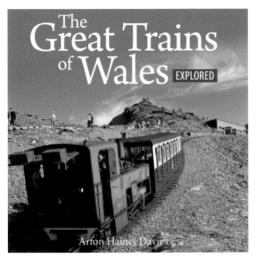

The Great Trains of Wales EXPLORED

Arfon Haines Davies

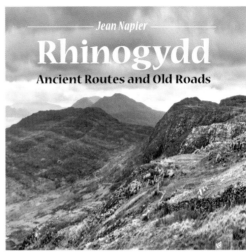

Jean Napier

Rhinogydd

Ancient Routes and Old Roads

Iconic Cycling

Trails in Wales

Phil Horsley

The Shepherd War Poet

Hedd Wyn
(Ellis H. Evans 1887-1917)
Introduction by Gruffudd Antur

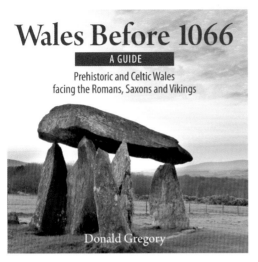

Wales Before 1066

A GUIDE

Prehistoric and Celtic Wales
facing the Romans, Saxons and Vikings

Donald Gregory

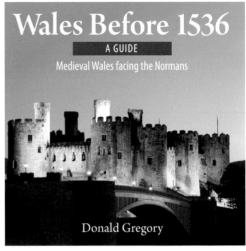

Wales Before 1536

A GUIDE

Medieval Wales facing the Normans

Donald Gregory

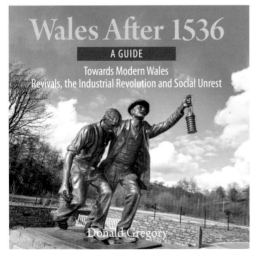

Wales After 1536

A GUIDE

Towards Modern Wales
Revivals, the Industrial Revolution and Social Unrest

Donald Gregory

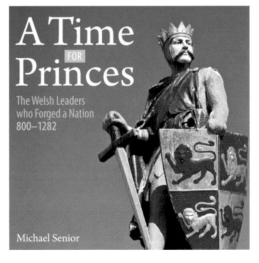

A Time FOR Princes

The Welsh Leaders
who Forged a Nation
800–1282

Michael Senior

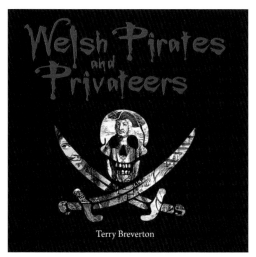

Welsh Pirates and Privateers

Terry Breverton

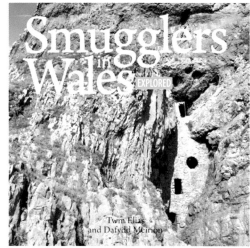

Smugglers in Wales EXPLORED

Twm Elias
and Dafydd Meirion

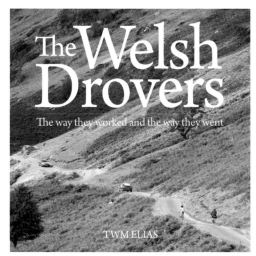

The Welsh Drovers

The way they worked and the way they went

TWM ELIAS

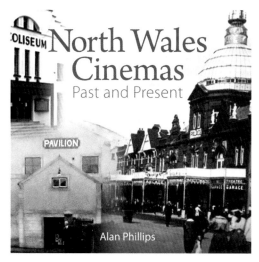

North Wales Cinemas
Past and Present

Alan Phillips